Tracks

The Piedmont Journal of Poetry & Fiction
2014 - 2018

Sara Brooks, Editor

PJPF Press

PiedmontJPF.com

These pieces are works of fiction or poetry. Names, characters, businesses, places, events and incidents are either the products of each author's imagination or used in a fictitious manner. Any resemblance to actual persons, living or dead, or actual events is coincidental.

ISBN 13 - 978-0-692-15738-1

ISBN - 0-692-15738-7

Cover design by Sara Brooks

Welcome to PJPF,

Four years ago, fresh from my college graduation, Milt Johns asked if I might be interested in editing for an online literary magazine, poetry web page, and general scribble factory. He was hoping to provide a decent platform for Virginia writers to showcase some of their works and a place where we might reach out to students, poets, and short story authors looking for that elusive first publication. He couldn't pay me but promised that I would be able to flex my recently-toned English literature muscles and that I'd get to work with mad scientist and sociopath, Robert Scott.

What followed was unexpected, but an enjoyable and emotional journey for me as I proceeded to receive brilliant submissions from writers all over the world. Poets, essayists, and fiction junkies sent me everything from rants to creative non-fiction to epic poems told in rhyming couplets (not kidding – check out Scott Howard's stuff.) I could barely keep up and often posted much-awaited editions weeks late. Thankfully, the writers with whom I was working remained understanding and forgiving, so I pressed onward, balancing my day job editing egregiously bad writing for the federal government with PJPF submissions. I knew I was hooked when I read Mitchell Grabois's, *I serve ice cream to children. It's my job. Even with my PhD, it was the best I could get.*

I remember thinking, "I love these people. They're like me. We're all just in here telling the truth together."

Four years later, we're still at it. The *Piedmont Journal of Poetry & Fiction* hasn't made fifty cents, but that's alright. I've corresponded with dozens of writers whose work often leaves me speechless. The journal has evolved into what I hope is an innovative collection of writings coupled with introspective, powerful photography, like wine with food, that refines and enriches the depth and meaning of each piece we publish. If you haven't visited the PJPF, check it out at *www.piedmontjpf.com*. The pieces featured in this collection have either been showcased on the site or are publications we've completed as side projects together. I hope you enjoy them all.

Until our next edition,

Sara Brooks, Editor

Contributing Writers

Bryan Harvey

Children Born of a Pacific Marriage

Because I lack scales
and no coral knots protrude
my spine, you would
never know how I am
Godzilla's heir.

Lured by a Golden Gate of digitalia,
my father moved to San Francisco
on Giant shoulders and mastered
the searing white art of raiding tablecloth seas:

he knew how to order sushi—
yellowtail, pink salmon, and
Sony's spicy tuna. Imperialism
tastes like raw fish; almed flesh
wrapped in a purse of avocado
and rice.

Mother was an orphan of defeat,
and the possibility exists,
despite what medals say,
that our grandfather murdered
her parents in a rain of salt
and fire. And, to this day,
she will not speak to us in Japanese,
choosing rather to read the subtitles
out loud and with no accent.

Still, my siblings and I learned how to scuffle
with the staffs of blind monks
dueling in our hands, opening
and closing like pigeons' beaks.
We washed over an archipelago
of porcelain, craning a fisherman's
netted labors from table to mouth
on the wings of foreign utensils:
tempura televisions and *Pokemon* ugani.

We ate with great appetites, but none
greater than our father's—

While consuming the raw fruits of the sea,
the big lizard roared as if the parallel currents
of hostility and pleasure were born from divine winds.

He devoured everything in scenes of cinematic gratuity.
Our bellies mushroomed, but his, the largest of all,
inspired a gluttonous guilt, with an aftertaste
of pride. And we, the offspring of his tradewind
breath and our mother's silent scars,
are a very Pacific species of mutation,
belched from love and war, intertwined by
a whirlwind of blood and fire. We cannot
speak its name. We can only speak the quakes
of its hunger; a roaring in our veins.

The First Twinkie

Mom raised us to be good eaters;
ascetic monks with temples
rising in our rib cages.
Carrots and celery were acceptable snacks—
peanut butter on apples,
if we were lucky—
ants crawling down our throats
like grains of sand
on a sacred beach.
We ate no different
than cavemen
before the use of fire,
before sharp sticks even.
We ate from gardens
and organic grocery aisles—
the scent of yoga mats
and the flavors of *ohm*.

However, when Mom laid out a
mandala of fruits and veggies,
Ronnie responded, "no thank you,

I brought a Twinkie."
We looked at the caked phallus
as space food, as some rocket
flying into the orbs of our beings,
like some Vulcan mind meld,
or fluorescent light saber.
When mom left the kitchen,
Ronnie slithered another
from his pocket.

I fumbled with the plastic—
ended up tearing it with my teeth—
until the sugary flesh
flooded my mouth
with pure
        unadulterated
perversion.

Assassination of a Silverback

The M-16 ruptured blood vessels—
red novas and shooting stars.
Each drop a comet streaking;
each drop a mark of extinction.
The body sagged like a mountain
under the weight of heavy weather,
gravity
        and time.
Fur thick and warm as jungle mist
covered the beast, except for where
 the bullets cratered into flesh.

Even in death, the creature seemed
almost human; pupils exposed
in mirrors of Adam

   .

The villagers lifted the gorilla
onto a stretcher, while arms
boughed in the muddy path,
soaking up the storm,
the lightning in the dirt.

They buried him as the sun set,
while his killers snorted *brown brown*,
      exhaled cigarettes,
            and cackled in the passing—

Azreal in the breeze
      like the buzzing of a fly
at a crimson-crested banquet—

Shooting stray rounds into the damp
belly of the sky,
they mimicked a kingly walk
and, under the pink light of constellations,
pounded stone knuckle to wooden chest
      and bellowed in the fog.

Nothing But Net

Galaxies collapse in a fold of nylon feathers,
only to be born again, to start over
with an orange teardrop, sphere-
shaped,

falling with gravity into the hands
of an exuding midwife,
some downtrodden
defender, who
will cradle
the ember
of a single
atom—

bounce it—

and let it go

Bryan Harvey lives in Virginia with his wife and two daughters. His poetry and fiction appear in *The Florida Review*, *The Cold Mountain Review*, *Bluestem Magazine*, *The Harpoon Review*, and *The Rufous City Review*. He blogs for Fansided's *The Step Back* and *The Classical* and is the creator of *Everything That Dunks Must Converge* and *With the Memphis Blues Again*. Feel free to follow him on Twitter @Bryan_S_Harvey. His dream is to one day eat scrambled pterodactyl eggs for breakfast.

(Which, to us, seems reasonable.)

Patricia Daly-Lipe

A Poetic Meditation

On this earth, there is oneness.
A rhythmic flow, a great symphony that is life.
Trees with roots, stems and leaves
Shells, fins, furs and wings, all living things.
Each has a purpose and to each, an end
And then . . .a new beginning.

Let us recapture the imagination of a child
See once more the mystery, beauty and joy of God
Playing within and behind, beyond and above.
Unite with the intimacy of commitment.
Trust takes time
But the gift is there . . .waiting.

Creativity

Planetary progress is being made,
So-called progress called technology.
But there is another path toward progress:
Creativity, the caring core of psychology.
Creativity cannot be ignored
Nor can it be disguised.
Become beguiled by your subconscious,
It cannot be contrived.
For every creative endeavor,
There is a spiritual side
Since the source of inspiration
Can never be denied.

Let thoughts flow as a current of compassion,
Believe the unbelievable, accept with satisfaction.
Yet creative imagination is but a part,
Since all intuitive collections come
From a place deep inside: the heart.

Les Pierres de Lacoste

A tapestry of stone,
Texture, tone, contrast
Converging, conveying
Linear patterns, cool and warm,
Light dancing upon and between,
Rough and smooth, cut, split,
Dusty.

Conflict tends to connect
The intimacy of hate,
The tension of love.

Stones everywhere: above, below,
Between.
Cobblestones weaving through centuries
As generations stumble.

Defense, design, fortress, home.

Hurry up, now, it's time, it's time!

Stoically, the tapestry of stone
Stands still.

Patricia Daly-Lipe was born in California, but spent an equal amount of time living in Washington, D.C. She graduated from Vassar College (with a year at the Catholic University of Louvain, Belgium) earning a B.A. degree in Philosophy. Later, with a Ph.D., Patricia taught English and writing, wrote for the *Evening Star* Newspaper and *La Jolla Village News*, and had stories published in several magazines. Patricia is the author of eight books, each a different genre. In 2017, she received the trophy from IAOTP (International Association of Top Professionals) for "lifetime of achievement and success."

Visit her online at: www.literarylady.com.

William Doreski

Cannibal-Sized Cook Pots

Your yard sale features cannibal
sized cook pots, tough black iron,
and the complete apparatus
of a still your father ran for years.
I'm not interested in boiling
my neighbors, and can't compete

with Kentucky or Tennessee
for bourbon, but I could plant
sunflowers in a pot and run
that alcoholic tubing across
the forest border to discourage
marauding white-tail deer.

You claim I'm too impractical
to carry out these schemes so
refuse to sell me anything,
even the bible your father
wielded like a mace. Inscribed
to his patron angel, this vast

folio always opens at Job.
Still, I want a cook pot and half
a mile of plastic tubing.
You with your withered red hair
and clattering old-fashioned grin
aren't the witch you pretend to be.

You cast all your spells at once,
at the moment of puberty
You left nothing to ripen
in the galvanized years that followed.
Now that your father has died,
leaving obscene manuscripts,

you hope some passing stranger
will carry forth his program
of pickling devils in alcohol

and displaying them in church.
Light pools and thickens in the pots.
Tiny voices course through the tubing

and emerge in titters. Please take
my money, and maybe later
a dose of real bourbon will douse
the memory of your fatal smile,
which in my own gray puberty
seared like bacon on a grill.

The Hittites Lived So Long Ago

A half mile from the Black Sea
you lounge and tan in your yard.
Cruise ships gloat in the harbor.
A rail line chuffs toward Russia

with smug diesel effort towing
white tank-car loads of chemicals.
You've lived here long enough
to forget how America shapes

nature to fuel its contentment.
I'm here to see the Hittite ruins,
the local museum with bronze
and ceramic shards, the ancient road

still paved with rutted limestone.
I didn't expect you to recall
our dazed afternoon in Vermont
lying exhausted in bed while children

percolated in meadow grass
and deer from the Taconics browsed
in the abandoned orchards behind
your rented house. Now in Turkey,

a woman living alone, you fret
about nothing. You lack wrinkles,
despite your age, and your body
shines like a Richard Serra sculpture.

As we chat about old times the trains
rasp along their uneven track
and a foghorn snorts in the harbor.
The Hittites never saw women

like you, but your Islamic neighbors
wave and greet you with cheerful bursts
of Arabic, which you return
with local accent. The Hittites

lived so long ago the planet
barely recalls their presence.
It won't remember us at all,
but the sparks we used to generate

lit up much of the unknown world.
Too bad we never explored it.
The chemical cars rattle and clank
and the salt-smell flavors our talk.

When I leave to visit the ruins
I'll retain the impress of your pose
and impose it on the ancient rubble
like a dusty sun-colored kiss.

On Silver Lake

You accuse me of herding
with creatures of the same bulk
and hide. You say that like sheep
and cattle I conceal myself
against predators by blending
into a background so dull
it stifles the spark of drama
that triggers hunger and the hunt.
No wonder that living risk-free
I've failed to excite the masses.
No wonder my scant publications
haven't banned me from Russia
or China, where cover stories count.

Autumn light relaxes on the lake
in various earth tones. You dare me
to steal a rowboat moored behind
a cottage shut for the season
and row you across the lake
to picnic with lobster rolls and wine.
But like Wordsworth I fear rebuke
of mountains, and confess that feeling
herd-ish I'd rather stay ashore
and have coffee at the general store.
You weren't serious about the boat,
but you do find me sheepish,
readily shorn. Not really bovine,
though, lacking that leathery stance
that braces itself against the glare
and casts a muscular shadow.

The creatures with whom I herd
are absent at the moment. Later
we'll gather to discuss a novel
or film or *The Basement Tapes*
of Bob Dylan and The Band.
You won't join us. The herding
instinct has never touched you,
so mocking it comes easily—
the earth tones of the lake-light
distorting reflections overlaid
with ripples the color of brains.

The Nile in Flood

Sometimes ancient Egypt
crushes me, three millennia
of stone, gold, and painted wood.
This morning the rain smells
like the Nile. The Nile in flood,
before the Aswan Dam ruined

the natural flood cycle behind
five thousand years of farming.
I'm talking of trivial things:
mummies and dog-faced statues,
stone sepulchers and bronze tools,
the earliest forms of glass.

The annual flood rendered works
of culture insignificant,
reclaiming by re-silting the land.
I could stand some private re-silting,
although the mess in the kitchen
would dismay my family. Blue

breaks over the desert, a deep blue
that threatens to drown millions
in glare so brazen it topples
anyone unprepared. But here
the winter rain snuffs ambitions,
and the new year promises to dry

our tears and replace them with stones,
gemstones of blue and green.
I didn't dream about Egypt.
I don't have to. Its deadweight
has dragged along behind me
all of my life, and the prayers

rendered to leathery useless gods
have stuck in my throat and stopped me
from swallowing larger doctrines
that with their larger instincts
would have freed me to walk in rain
without getting my carcass wet.

The Last Thrush

You smudged my paint job, slurred
the perfect enamel I layered
on my favorite stick of furniture.

No pomp of speech can resolve
this insult. No manner of cloud
can occlude your guilty pleasure.

The last of summer's thrushes
dangles a bit of song, then wheels
south with ambitions unfulfilled.

A pond of giant carp withdraws
into its mud bath, the fish dreaming
those dreams we reserved for ourselves

when we briefly owned the cosmos.
Not much play left in machinery
grinding itself into chaos.

Not much data left unfiled.
You enjoy smearing the paint
because Milton and Stevens

and even your hero, Melville,
abraded their patient wives.
Your fingerprints will testify

that imperfections precede me
into whatever next world I step
when oblivions blurs starlight

and voids the most recent eclipse.
Your disdain of Milton fails
to note his elegiac youth

when the great moments claimed him
in spangles of ruminant Latin.
Your distrust of Stevens ignores

the one of fictive music who moves
still on the same waters on which
you walk with insolent glee.

As for Melville: your quotations
from *Moby-Dick* seems ersatz,
but I'm too tired to research

and convict you of insolence
you already flaunt. The last thrush
percolates past the horizon

and leaves a smoke-trail of song
credible as a blues tune hacked
from a lone disgruntled chord.

William Doreski lives in Peterborough, New Hampshire. He has published three critical studies. His poetry has appeared in many journals. He has taught writing and literature at Emerson, Goddard, Boston University, and Keene State College. His new poetry collection is *A Black River, A Dark Fall* (2018).

Barbara Buckley Ristine

It's election night and I hear the voice of the people

The candidate can't contain his glee:
the people have spoken, he is anointed.
A reporter remarks on his populist appeal.

Populist, *populous, populares, vox populi vox Dei.*
People, We the People, just plain folks.

Our desires summoned him,
we believed he was truly ours,
ours to command.
He wears the worker's ragged jacket,
rolls up his sleeves, just one of the guys.
We're all the same, he tells us.
His words mirror our thoughts,
he reminds us of our terror
as he promises to deliver us,
to satisfy our craving.

We've had this dream before.
The populists wore the people's face.
Peron, Chavez, Long, Wallace.
Our creations.
I'm just like you, they shouted.
Your voice has been ignored too long.
Blame the others, the outsiders,
they've taken what's yours.
The people demanded their due.

Nights of broken glass,
we hear the smash of clubs,
the snap of bones as they break.
Victorious, his mask is lifted,
he doesn't need the people's face now.
The people have spoken,
Vox populi vox Dei
our new god speaks with fire,
wears a brown shirt, wears a white hood.

3 A.M.

The crash of metal,
the squeal of rubber on concrete,
the smash of flesh hitting glass
faded from the night,
I arrived, camera in hand.
The smoke cleared and I saw her,
slumped in the seat,
the life drained out.
I felt the ground shake
as the heavy footed medic
rolled the gurney past.
Blue lights glittered
 in glass scattered
on blacktop.
White head lights
danced across her shattered face
frozen in a scream.

Gleaning

I've avoided
the garden.
Its disorder and
chaos reproach me.

Yellowing leaves,
fallen branches,
overgrown weeds,
reminders of my neglect.

But today I yielded,
drawn by the
scarlet peeking out
from green weeds

yellow pear tomatoes
showing off their gold,

shy peppers hiding
with the squash.

I pull the tiny
scarlet orbs from
bent stems,
careful not to squeeze.

No basket at hand
I stuff the gleanings
into the hem of my shirt
stained with their juice.

I hear the hawk
screeching overhead.
The harvest does not
interest him.

He's waiting for
stupid fat doves.

Paradise (Still) Lost

We tried without success
to curate our nostalgia,
To reframe it
 into something sublime.

Instead, we created
a version of the past
 gilded with fools' gold.

We could not say
what went wrong.
We only knew
that we had fallen
from grace.

We tried to make
a past perfect.
But all we did
was cultivate anarchy.

Barbara Buckley Ristine started her professional life as an attorney, but finally realized that writing is more fun. Her work has appeared or is forthcoming in *The Meadow, Literally Stories, The Magnolia Review,* and *Brushfire Literature & Arts Journal.*

She lives in northern Nevada where she occasionally blogs about life and writing at www.mydearestcassandra.wordpress.com.

Fabrice Poussin

Long after the ball

The crash is loud as it echoes through even the spirit strong;
by the window, the old shack barely enough to safety;
dressed in poverty she stands, fingers to the damp glass,
a dusty curtain greets her with memories of many scores.

She blinks again as fire possesses the air otherwise so serene;
the insides no longer calm, a heartbeat no longer pleased,
she shivers in fear of what may enter, what she does not know;
knees do not consider the effort, they need to disconnect.

Body blinded unreal with another flash, life could leave;
hanging to the frame of what was once a dearly home,
the soul wants to play, needs to laugh, grab onto what once was;
run to the trees, rod begging for a jolt powerful, luminous.

The eye of terror asks for a reprieve collapsing in the now;
salty the river runs; as the loss seems certain the heart explodes;
hands feel a place there was once life new, immeasurable the pain;
brow to the glass freezing, she looks for a chance to dim the fever.

No light indoors, she wonders of the end since nightmare rules;
she fears, alone, light is armed with jagged daggers and swords;
her survival is optional only, for there is no knight in sight;
like the earthquake that swallows all, lightning again.

Child, little girl, woman, naught has changed for yesteryear;
pray to your hope, dream farther, all will be well indeed;
in morn' again, reborn you will love, when day comes,
lady of the ball, dance, dance in light, you are safe.

Summer with ghosts

It was not so long ago that you walked in the mud,
tightening up your belt with an old hemp rope,
whistling your newest tune, as the swallows pondered.

Six summers have cooled since you last preserved
seasons of endless bounties in glass jars.

Then you could still enjoy the scents of your creations,
when the flame gently gave life to a great repast.

Soon again, I will risk another step into the halls
of a museum erected by your weary palms,
alone in a forest of icons, guarding my spirit
as for the first time, it is your soul I will meet.

Perhaps, warming near your old companion,
you hold hands in an eternity you possess.

Will you see me, as I enter your private realm,
recognize me, once the questioning child,
accept my presence near you within your wall?

Everyday the same query will surface on my lips,
seeking with my gaze for a sign of your love
on the seals, crannies, everything you once touched,
vulnerable, in the midst of the unknown.

It must in be in the comfort of ages that you make
a cocoon, to protect those who dare still to
love the ghosts of your missing embrace.

Night and the Spirit

Night has come on her swift legs to surprise the maiden,
sleeping on the rock overlooking a great many souls;
the spirit cupped in the deep of her curved palms,
simply sitting fearless in uncertain boundaries.

Lifting her chin to the darkness which envelops
her whole being like a shroud of living hope true,
where one is crushed in heaviest confusion;
she stands slowly asserted with the power of all.

In her eyes, sister of Phoebus shines faint it seems;
source of life extended beyond the might of day;

not so says she, gray perhaps in others' view
infinite in tones to her, the chord is ever strong.

Through the wave above, the shine grows greater
into the mind of the one who knows and feels;
the source of an ever reaching road of many
paths unbeatable, young, teenager, adult, old.

She knows no death with her heavenly accomplice;
lifting her gaze to a sister deeply loving, caring,
against a somber backdrop of night and cruel mysteries;
regrouping onto her center the fire burns exquisite.

On the rock so dear, no need to stir a fiber living;
up, gray, endowed with a dim jealous glimmer from the day;
a mere wink encourages delight to her awesome cohort,
peace to the goddess, all is well all around, you may sleep now.

Old Boy

He raises his hand with a question
to a giant in a pleaded skirt of plaid;
dwarf in his crushed little heart down under,
wondering why today he still cries.

But the lady looks up to the dwarf oddly,
as if the colossus was he, and she the child,
yet no mistake is there, neither he,
nor she is gander than the other.

Little boy in wrinkles, old man with baby skin,
she, a goddess of dark and blue, wonders
why he whimpers, terrified pup,
as only the sun shines in the firmament.

It is hard growing into that masterful elder,
when always, he comes home alone,
and the night remains a sole experience;
he will never age, outsider he will remain.

Embrace

On a sad dreary day, you made a gift to me,
a present of your breast to mine in earnest,
the imprint of a scar in the shape of the lines
your body carves on the world you know.

Thankful I have walked since, comforted,
ever as I may close these eyes, and relapse
into the power of those nurturing arms;
you so strongly wrapped around my pain.

A gift like no other, simple, so remarkable,
upon a return to a world changed forevermore,
at an appointed time, as if one was needed,
you stood, the little girl who still refuses to age.

Better than Mona Lisa, you showed your peace;
the moment continues yet, and there standing,
something fell once, and again, then again,
electrons shot through those silly nerves giddy.

No bow, no fancy carton, a present always,
as your body arched, a step away, and aside,
the air moved with your infinite rhythm, jolly,
to this day, humbled, I know its vibrancy.

Not a physical entity, but so much more,
hovering like a dust of innumerable selves,
with the ability to share all, you are in all,
I thus must give praise to your soul aglow.

Fabrice Poussin teaches French and English at a small liberal arts university.
Author of novels and poetry, his work has appeared in *Kestrel*, *Symposium*,
Eskimo Pie, *The Chimes* and other magazines. His photography has been
published in *The Front Porch Review*, *Foliate Oak Magazine*, *San Pedro River
Magazine* and dozens of others. Living in Northern Georgia, he often travels
to Europe. Always working on a project, he hopes that his endeavors into
another dimension of photography will be appreciated by the viewers (a
mystery for now). When not photographing, he expresses himself in poetry.

Garrett Carlson

Pickled Herring and the Christmas Dream

It was a Carlson family tradition every year for Christmas, if you were to bring a new significant other to the table they must try to eat a piece of pickled herring. It was some sort of strange rite of passage if you were able to finish the tar-colored fish, you'd be welcomed into the family. To this day my mom still complains about how she was forced to garble it down without throwing up.

When my last girlfriend came over for Christmas Eve, I made sure to keep this part of the deal secret. I didn't know what she was capable of (apparently vague threats of murder was something definitely in her wheelhouse). After a brief moment of gift-giving under the tree, she was finally informed that she had to eat the herring. I tried to play it off like I had no idea this was something that we did, or some new family tradition, but that didn't really get me far when my great-grandmother informed my current ex-girlfriend about how my last ex-girlfriend refused to even look at the fish. Thanks Evelyn, you're great fucking support.

With anger being drawn from being compared to my last ex-girlfriend (who was definitely better and had less murderous tendencies), and being forced to eat this foul smelling meal, she decided we were going to need to have one of those silent conversations that most couples tend to have only in moments when real danger is imminent.

Her: "What is this? It smells horribly."

Me: "It's pickled herring. I don't know where it came from. I don't know how long it was alive for and I don't know if it is fully dead. I do know that if you want to be a part of the Carlson Carnival, you'll have to eventually finish it."

(Let me briefly interrupt by saying I really did not want her to finish it)

Her: "My family didn't make you eat any of this, we had ham. And potatoes."

Me: "And of course you won't let me forget it will you. And the potatoes you had at your dinner were red and brown and gross. Can you please just eat the herring, a tiny nibble or something?"

Her: "You eat the goddamned herring, Garrett."

I thought the vein in her forehead was going to explode into my eyes and they would eventually match the holiday-colored tablecloth. She grabbed the knife next to her fork and for the briefest of seconds, I thought she was actually going to eat the herring. Now I think she was half thinking, "Can I stab him in the chest and get out of here without getting caught? Probably not. I'll play the long con instead, send him some passive-aggressive emails letting him know his town isn't big enough for the both of us. I like that idea more. Then I'll murder him."

Listen, it isn't slander if it's true. If this story ever gets printed and I go missing, Ice T better begin the investigation of my disappearance at her house. I'm not saying this is a cry for help that she will murder me when I am back in Buffalo, but I am saying it is not out of the realm of possibility at this point.

Thankfully she didn't end up eating the herring, and I can guarantee you that I am about 50% sure that's not why we broke up.

Now this year, with two empty seats next to me, my great-grandmother now passed on, and the other left open for whoever is brave enough next to meet my family, I understand that these little traditions are so important. That's why the next girl who sits beside me at the table will have to eat the pickled herring . . . and not shed any of my blood.

26 Miles and Counting

Outside the Irish Channel bar in Chinatown, a tall man wearing a skin-tight black Under Armour shirt wandered in. Adorned to his chest was his race number, and around his neck was his participation medal. This jerk ran his hand through his wavy hair and released his pheromones into the Irish wilderness. The women next to us melted as he looked at them and loudly told the man next to him:

"I just love to run, I mean, my goal is to run a marathon in all 50 states."

No, I am serious. That is an exact quote that came out of his mouth and by God did it work. Now I had no reason not to believe him, but did he have to rub it in all the other people's faces like that?

And with that, a horrible idea was born.

We left the Channel and back to James's apartment where I proudly announced I was going to run the Rock'N'Roll Marathon in D.C. To prove it to them, I went on James's laptop, paid the fees, and registered as a participant in a marathon. My logic (which there seems to be none) was that if I paid the money, there was no way in hell I would let it go to waste.

I woke up the next day, got ready for work, and soon realized that I was going to have to run a marathon.

26 miles.

42.195 kilometers.

1,647,360 inches.

There were multiple problems with this situation, like the fact that I was not a runner. In fact, my athletic expertise exists solely in recreational sports that aren't sports to begin with. I have a three-way tie for the greatest athletic achievement of my life.

When I was 13, I was forced to take part in a karate tournament. Now I had been around the block a few times when it comes to getting into rumbles, but the consensus was that I was going to get my rear-end kicked. That's when the karate gods gave me my first break. The age cutoff needed to be changed the day of so at 13 years of age, I was now the oldest member of my group. When the tournament started, I began scouting out my competition and to be honest; I felt pretty good about my chances.

That was until an 11-year-old monster named Renee showed up. Everyone watching just chuckled at the thought of this tiny, petite girl in pink karate attire stepping into the circle to challenge the boys. No one chuckled after she broke her first opponent's nose in eight seconds. In fact, her next opponent told his mom that he wanted to forfeit. If she listened, she wouldn't have had to pay for hospital bills to repair ANOTHER BROKEN NOSE.

The karate gods decided to give me my second break when the official judges found Renee's forceful contact a bit much and disqualified her from the rest of the tournament. It just so happened that I was next in line, and I ended up walking out of there holding a first place karate tournament trophy that I brought home, put away in a closet, and never spoke of again in case Renee could somehow hear me. I saw Final Destination; you can only cheat death so many times.

My high school sporting career was limited to two years of amateur wrestling (no, there are absolutely no pictures of me in a singlet, don't even try to find one), and professional dodgeball. Alright, maybe it wasn't professional, but it was pretty close to it. Along with seven of my closest friends, we decided that we weren't athletic enough for real sports, but what kind of people actually would show up for a dodge ball league right?

Wrong. Again. We were manhandled by nearly every team we played, and when the playoffs came, the outlook was bleak. That was until a massive snowstorm hit rendering out four of the five best players in the league's cars inoperable and we somehow accidentally found ourselves in third place. Our team didn't get a trophy, but we did get some nice t-shirts. (And yes, I still wear my t-shirt. A lot.)

I am a two-time Fantasy Football champion.

I get it, the third one isn't an athletic achievement but based on the first two, can you just give it to me?

But in any of those events, did I mention running at all? Of course, I didn't because I am not a runner. Literally, the only time I ever ran was if I was being chased, and despite being on the wrestling team, or on a dodgeball team, or whatever other embarrassing stories I've already written about, I was not chased often. I was now signed up for run 26 miles. In a row. All at once.

I needed to train, and I did. I trained for real. I set up a running schedule, I went to the gym, I busted my butt. I even dated a girl for a few months who ran races for fun while dressing in costume. That wasn't the reason we dated, but I am sure that was fate's reason for why we broke up.

My weekends were designed around my runs and two weeks before the big race I pushed myself for 24 miles, which I completed. I didn't move off my couch for the next 36 hours, but I did it, and surprisingly it felt really good. There was a chance I could do it. That's where I was wrong, dead wrong.

A week before the race, my friend in the city posted on Facebook about the St. Patrick's Day Leprechaun Leap 8K. I had no plans for the weekend, and I figured why the hell not, it was only an 8k. I could do this in my sleep. We made plans to meet up, I paid my fees, got my shirt, I was ready to go.

With the wind blustering, I got into starting position near my friend and waited. Hundreds upon hundreds of people were lined up alongside me ready to run this race. Listen, I wasn't looking to get first place, I just wanted to beat my friends time, and as the race went on, I was doing well. I was keeping pace with everyone, drinking water like a champ, slamming my plastic cup on the ground as if I was saying, "HOLD UP PEOPLE, I DON'T HAVE TIME TO CARRY THIS CUP BECAUSE I AM RUNNING WAY TOO FAST!"

Now the next part is going to be truly embarrassing. I don't know if it's more or less embarrassing than everything else I've told you, but it isn't a good thing.

Right around the 3rd mile or so, the world seemed to be in order. My music was great; my legs felt wonderful, thirst was quenched. That is until I saw that goddamned gingerbread man.

I never realized running races in costume was so popular, but to be fair, who am I to judge, I actively play wiffleball, a sport designed for 8-year-olds. I have to say, though; there was just something about this gingerbread man racing past me that made me furious. My face red, the fury building, I told my body to step it up a notch. I would have been fine getting my nose broken by an 11-year-old girl in a karate tournament, I would have been fine getting the last place in a dodge ball tournament, but I would rather die than be outrun by someone dressed as a gingerbread man.

My legs started churning, faster and faster and faster until I was at pace with the gingerbread man. As we ran, I glanced over at him and just snarled. Not like a dog per se, but not entirely like a human being either. We can both agree it wasn't the finest of moments for me. Footstep for a footstep, we were together. Nothing was going to separate me from my goal of beating this damn gingerbread man. Well, there was one thing. The pothole near 13th Street.

I was so busy staring down this gingerbread man that I failed to look down at where I was running. This was Final Destination coming to get me once and for all as my foot sunk into the hole and in slow motion, my entire body hit the pavement. I glanced up; the gingerbread man turned his head, and I swear if I could have seen through that mask, we would have seen him smiling at my misery.

Eventually, I hobbled my way across the finish line only to drive back home that night with a swollen ankle. The next day I tried jogging but there was no use, I couldn't put any pressure on my foot. It seemed as if my dreams of being a marathon runner were over.

Despite not being able to run, I still went to D.C. the weekend of the race to visit my friends. I never went and picked up my free marathon t-shirt, but thankfully my good friend picked one up for me after she completed it herself. I threw it on and forgot all about it.

That afternoon, there was a crowd returning home from a St. Paddy's themed event on the Orange Metro line home.

I have always been one who believed in destiny and that I would meet the woman of my dreams on the train. After seeing the debauchery on the train this night, I hope she wasn't. There were people dressed as leprechauns making out; hell I saw one person vomiting near the emergency exit door.

The entire train ride home, I tried to ignore the people around me to have a silent conversation with the cute girl in front of me. One of the problems with a silent conversation is that no one is talking, so I resigned myself to staring out through the window until my stop.

An announcement over the loud speaker: "Last stop, Vienna." Doors opened, and we all made our way towards the exit when I felt a tap on my shoulder. It was the girl sitting across from me.

"Excuse me, did you run the race this morning?"

Remember, I'm weak-willed around women I'm attracted to.

"Yeah, absolutely. Actually, I'm trying to run a marathon in all 50 states."

Facts about Owls

The average life of a wild adult barn owl is four years. That means today, less than a month away from being 30, I have survived 7.5 barn owl life spans. Except for Bernard "The British" Barn Owl, he endured 15 years before Brexit-ing himself off this Earth.

I like to imagine the life of a barn owl to be one filled with purpose. Subconsciously, in their brains, they recognize that they only have so many years to live, so they learn to fly. There is no time for tedious walking and sightseeing; barn owls have places to be, voles to eat, lollipop puzzles to answer.

Yes, that is a Tootsie Pop joke.

Two years ago on Rachel and I's first date, we were trudging through the Alexandria Wetlands. Still unsure if our hands fit together, we settled for her arm around my stomach when I stopped and looked up. Perched atop a tree was an owl.

Wildlife biologist John Powers said "When Europeans arrived in North America they brought most of their negative feelings regarding owls with them. Few of their positive beliefs seem to have made the crossing...In general, European Americans considered owls to be birds of ill omen." On the other hand, the rye stored for bread in Europe was often infected with ergot, an LSD-esque fungus that caused hallucinations, gangrene, and death.

So maybe we should hold off on trusting the same people who believed that if you owned a cat, you were likely a witch.

The truth is that most scientists believe that owls are an indicator of a healthy, natural order to the world around them. They are a sign of wisdom and knowledge.

I believe that seeing that owl on that April afternoon meant something important; it was a symbol of happiness and healthiness. But also, the next evolution of myself as a human being.

As I've been getting older, the fragility of my own life has been slowly creeping in. When I was 22 years old, my diet consisted of Lucky Charms cereal in the morning, a Buffalo Chicken Finger sub in the afternoon, and usually two dinners with at least one of them being pizza. Sometimes if I were lucky, both would be pizza.

Now, 2 barn owl lives later; I am beginning to recognize that my metabolism is starting to slow down. At the age of 25, your metabolism begins its decline, sometimes as much as 2-4% per year. I was used to being super thin for all my life until probably the last six months or so.

I feel like every piece of pizza lays in my stomach for hours. The idea of 2 McDonald's cheeseburgers, a large fry, and a spicy chicken sandwich at 11 P.M. on a Tuesday used to sound heavenly. If I were to try that tonight though, I'd wake up tomorrow so bloated I'd begin walking with a hunch to prevent the pain of my lower abdomen from getting worse. And don't get me started on the weird gassy noises coming from my body every time I am trying to teach in class.

As for alcohol, I can't even drink one of my shitty watered down Canadian beers without getting heartburn. Which might be the oldest person sentence I have ever written.

But ignoring my newly-minted body image issues, I've begun to recognize that there is beauty in looking at life through the eyes of the barn owl.

I mean, imagine knowing that you had only four years total, from birth until death. I know that I wouldn't still be holding onto so many petty grudges if my lifespan was that short. So maybe it might be time for me to begin forgiving.

Starting with Geoff Crossley. I no longer hate you for ignoring me on the bus on our first day of middle school. Middle school kind of sucks, so I get it that you were trying hard to impress Samantha. She was after all the cutest girl on Bus 179. Geoff Crossley, you have been forgiven.

Dave Matthews and his band, I no longer hold a grudge against you for inspiring a bunch of college burnouts to go live in a van and follow you around on tour. I also no longer blame you for making Frisbee a competitive sport and single handily bringing back the hacky sack.

Besides, I must admit in my old age; I've begun to dig your crunchy grooves.

Angela Lansbury, star of Murder She Wrote, I no longer hate you for being the only show my grandmother would watch every summer afternoon. Angela Lansbury, I should also note that I no longer have a weird crush on you.

Getting all of that off my chest makes me feel a lot better.

Barn owls are also notorious for their hearing ability. They have the ability to locate and capture prey by sound alone. Their sensitive hearing enhanced by the owl's facial ruff, a type of reflector that channels sound into the owl's ears.

They are patient listeners, something I could learn to be better at before I turn 30. We often listen just long enough to be able to respond to whomever we are talking to but to truly listen to means to have the willingness to change.

And at 29 and ¾ years old, I'm pretty damn stubborn.

I didn't listen to my mother when she told me not to wear my heart on my sleeve because she knew I was going to get hurt. I didn't listen to my father when he told me not to stick tweezers in the light socket because there would be no way for you to get away with it in front of your high school biology teacher. I didn't listen to my friends when they told me Jorts stopped being cool years ago.

I should have listened.

But there is just something about being young and this idea that we are always the smartest person in the room. I always believed that I knew everything.

And I've been proven wrong every single year. I wonder in my life would have changed if I had just listened to those who had more experience, more knowledge than me.

I could have been a better teacher, a better son, a better partner.

Barn owls don't have the luxury of learning from their mistakes. Every moment of their life is critical to their survival.

Last year, about a week before my birthday, Rachel and I celebrated with my friends Scott and Jill in Philadelphia. As we laid in bed, still slightly intoxicated from our speakeasy tour, I realized that this was going to be the last year I could use the excuse "I'm dumb because I'm in my twenties." Somewhere along the way, I also reflected on all that I learned over the previous nine years.

I learned that moving by yourself can be the scariest, loneliest, and most rewarding experience of your life. I learned that it is OK to admit that you are depressed and you need some help. I learned that for you to be in a healthy relationship, you need to communicate even when it is hard.

I learned the difference between being right and being righteous. I learned the difference between being in love with someone and being in love with a moment in time.

And now, I'm learning to reflect on what I get to learn in the future: What it's like to be a husband or a father, what it's like to be a homeowner, what it's like to start picking out gray hairs every morning before work.

I'd like to believe that for every barn owl life span we live, it's like a little mini-evolution of ourselves. We are born, we listen to the sounds on the ground, and we die. And it happens over and over again, but we continue to be reborn from our past lives with more knowledge.

We are significantly different from barn owls in that the average person lives 20 times longer. We have the time to learn from our mistakes, to continue evolving as a species. I'm currently on my 7th barn owl life, just a few weeks from 30. I count my blessings to be as alive as I am right now.

And as I counted my 13 gray hairs in my bathroom mirror this morning, I realized that I am not afraid of death, I am afraid of not evolving.

Since before Drake graduated from Degrassi, Garrett Carlson has been attempting to pen the next great American novel. (These pieces are not it.) Garrett resides in suburban Virginia where he spends his days educating the leaders of tomorrow and contemplating comedic timing. Garrett also enjoys long walks on Beaver Island State Park Beach, collecting refrigerator magnets, and recreating scenes from the *Fast and Furious* franchise. A regular at open-mic nights and writers' workshops, Garrett is constantly learning, improving, and gaining an understanding about the craft of writing. He hopes to someday travel around the world and be paid just to talk to people about what he has written.

Garrett is currently pursuing a Masters in Non-Fiction Writing from Johns Hopkins University. For news and updates, visit his website www.gmcarlson.com and follow him on Twitter @gmcarlsonwrite.

Jane Ellen Glasser

Recalling the Blue Ridge in Summer

Sunlit, a thousand tinctures of green.
Up, up through fretwork, a sparrow's
clanky phrases, a cardinal's flames.
Rustling a tulip poplar's leaves,
the question marks of a squirrel's tail.
Through shrubby interstices, the white
flags of skittish deer. Along a dirt trail,
hieroglyphic prints and steamy scat
of red fox, black bear. Rinsing the air,
the tiny mouths of violets. As if a name
could tame what's wild, black-eyed
Susan, bouncing Bet, butter and eggs,
Queen Anne's lace. Deep in shadow
where roots snake, like items dropped
in a fairytale, lady's slippers, Indian pipes.

Eden Cottage

Charlottesville, VA

Over clay and blue stone
the creek's song keeps going
thin in its dry throat.

The morning-wet grass
is seeded with sound,
a muted unwinding of gears.

Green backed with green
deepens in shadow.
Wind rustle. Bird chatter.

Now sound transmutes
to motion, as if song,
internalized, fuels the wings.

A golden finch lasers
a trajectory, hickory to feeder.
The air hums like a taut wire.

Beyond, July's uncut fields
dance to a reel that skirts
the registers of the human ear.

Turkey Buzzards

Wings uplifted in a V
they soar in wobbly circles,
riding thermals
to scan the countryside,

or steered by smell
they glide low,
their shadows gracing
pastures, dumpsters,
the black tablecloths
of highways.

A fresh kill
will draw a wake,
bald heads bobbing,
hooked bills tearing
into any sick
or breathless thing.

At night they retreat
to the skeletons
of hollow trees,
their only song a dirge
of grunts and hisses.

Autumn at Chesley Creek Farm

Morning by the creek
where red and yellow leaves float,
I startled a doe.

Beneath a blazed tree,
a patch of Indian pipes
hid from the noon sun.

On the porch at dusk,
I sipped a glass of claret
wrapped in a wool shawl.

At night while I slept,
a white river of moonlight
streamed into my dreams.

Jane Ellen Glasser's poetry has appeared in numerous journals, such as *Hudson Review*, *Southern Review*, *Virginia Quarterly Review*, and *Georgia Review*. In the past she reviewed poetry books for the *Virginian-Pilot*, edited poetry for *Ghent Quarterly* and *Lady Jane's Miscellany*, and co-founded the nonprofit arts organization and journal *New Virginia Review*. A first collection of her poetry, *Naming the Darkness*, with an introduction by W. D. Snodgrass, was issued by Road Publishers in 1991. She won the Tampa Review Prize for Poetry 2005 for *Light Persists* and *The Long Life* won the Poetica Publishing Company Chapbook Contest in 2011. *The Red Coat* (2013), *Cracks* (2015), and *In the Shadow of Paradise* (2017), are available from Future Cycle Press.

Visit her online at: www.janeellenglasser.com

Cassandra Parker

Landfill

Clean for a few weeks,
      dirty for months afterward—
When will I learn that you are not for keeps
          and force my head to turn forward?

At least we're Eco-friendly,
constantly reusing until there's nothing left at all…
      Maybe the environment is happy,
        but I am all Winter— no more Spring, Summer, or Fall.

Whoever wagered a future on this—
      think again—
it's not a long term solution.

Her needs are a landfill compared to his,
         but now her heart is sick of self pollution.

A Man is A Man is A Man

Sparks illuminate your three month beard
as your hand steers the cigarette to your lips.
The smoke curls around your head,
which is pounding from the poison
you've imbibed in so many forms.

I've stopped coming around.
Holding you up proved too heavy of a feat
to repeat every night each week.
If it's not the pills, it's the smokes,
and if it's not the smokes, it's the drink.

You take advantage of all in your path.
Even the sympathy dripping from our veins
becomes an abuse of power in your twisted mind.
You are turning black from the inside out,
but it's leaving me, drip by drip.

I've stopped coming, for you.
Your touch is cold, punishing, foreign.
The manliest part of the new you
is the fist you use to smash the things
that once meant so much to the both of us.

I've stopped coming around, yet.
I still think of you every day, worried,
wondering, when you've hurt us all
who will be left standing over you?
Him: the one you hate the most.

Echocardiography

Sonogram my heart
          To find scripted autographs
    Of lovers long gone

Take no mind to those
          Little nicks in the sinew
They'll heal in time

Cassandra Parker is freelance writing for all kinds of interesting characters and businesses these days. When she's not tucked away in her home office in Nokesville, Virginia with Imogen the Kitten, she's out on the football pitch!

Visit her online at CassandraParker.com.

Kathy Cable Smaltz

Part to Whole

Each year I find more of myself
up and down the banks of this river.

Ashamed of who I was back then,
I fileted myself like a fish, cut
through the flapping tail while
bulging eye stared, blade sliced
through spine and scales
then guts spilled out, heart
beating, bleeding, offering up
only the parts men told me they'd eat.

Over here behind the boat,
given up for you,
two bared breasts, no big deal
just teenage A cups with tender pink tips,
but they were mine and I peeled
them off, replaced with silicon
so someone would say he remembered me.

I once watched a friend filet
fish on his dock, the S shaped motion of the
knife, accusing eye watching,
I asked him why he let them
suffer like that
why he didn't behead them
first but he said fish don't suffer because
they don't know, and no one cuts the head
off if he knows what he's doing it's bloody
and wasteful, only done in cinema, better
the head and tail go down together
without their body into the chum bucket
or back into the river.

If you crouch on your hands and knees
under that cleaning table, you'll find my heart,
with all of its severed valves, just where I hid it

hoping, one day, to return for my broken treasure.

I no longer remember why these
faceless men mattered more to me
than I mattered to me
except my sense of self so shrunken from shame
I couldn't name, or know its source.

I miss that girl sometimes, the one
whose individual body parts, so lovely,
formed a whole so guileless to everyone
but her. She lives inside this older version
of me, inside my beating heart, my fingers, my
breasts, my stretch marked stomach,
my shoulders, my cheeks, my open eyes,
my one true body.

Sylvia, Oh Sylvia

Why were you baking cakes while Ted combed the beach?
Your desk empty … its view of white water rolling onto shore, foam
Swallowed by sand.

In the kitchen coated in flour, smelling of vanilla bean,
You greeted Ted with cakes, not poems.

Like puddles of water in sand after high tide, madness:
Postpartum. Insomnia. Depression.

Years later, reading your words, I wish I could save you:
Bound upstairs, bend over you, blow words into your breathless body.

I want to shake your shoulders and say, "Sylvia! You don't need Ted or any
man. Pick up your pen, push out more poems instead of babies who need
prams. Love the babes you have, go back to the door, and peel off that silly
tape.

Caress your youngest's cheek, climb into bed with your oldest.
Get. Some. Sleep."

In the morning, I would have squeezed fresh orange juice,
made toast, and told her:

"These black marauders come and go.
They're matchstick men and not your foe."

At Night the Killer in Darkness
(Auvillar, France, 2012)

Who found the knives
I placed in the French crock last night?
A subtle gesture, each blade brought
down off the magnetic board in darkness
a bit like tucking them in, so I, who am alone
do not wake in fear of being cut.

In America, intruders cut
the phone and electric lines and knife
people in their sleep, those alone
are most vulnerable at night,
where sociopaths love the darkness,
the intimate thrill it brings.

Those Florida college girls even brought
their boyfriends in, years ago, but the killer cut
all of them in the darkness
in a ground floor apartment in Gainesville, a knife
the weapon du jour and night
the perfect cloak for a killer acting alone.

I am afraid of sleeping alone,
and the airlines said no mace, so I bring
myself into the kitchen at night,
where the weak overhead bulb cuts
through black, and there – the knife.
Days ago, across the Atlantic's waves, grey and dark
I sat in my window seat, flew alone,
ate my sesame chicken with my plastic knife.
I didn't know I'd brought
along this killer like carry-on luggage, the predator cut
out from headlines, strongest at night.

I sleep better now at night
knowing that in the darkness
if I'm attacked, I too can cut:
eye, gut, heart of a killer, alone.
He won't be the only one who brought
with him the gleaming blade of a knife.

Once home again, on the news, killers will knife through the darkness
on my flat screen at night, but then I will not be alone
as the glare of our TV is brought into focus, then cut.

Mother, wife, and teacher, Kathy Cable Smaltz started writing by penning bad love poems in high school while listening to Richard Marx and Air Supply. Now that she's a feminist writer, she wishes she'd been more of a Pat Benatar fan.

Smaltz has published in various regional and national journals and for three years was the parenting columnist for *Bristow Beat*. She's earned honors from the Virginia Press Association, was PWC Poet Laureate from 2016-2018, is the recipient of a Mid-Atlantic Arts grant and a fellow with the Virginia Center for the Creative Arts.

(We love *Part to Whole*.)

Mitchell Grabois

Gravois

The universe is expanding nine percent faster than previously imagined. Dark energy is thought to be the cause. I could have told you that—I knew it as far back as when I lived in an Oakland flophouse and drank Ripple with my British buddy Marcel on the shores of Lake Merritt. Other times, at Bill McNally's Irish Pub, his old school tie would fall into our pitcher of beer, and when I pointed this out to him, he rewarded me with an insane grin and the observation that "We are shitfaced."

His girlfriend, Priscilla, was a porcine American. Our roommate was the last American male to contract polio. I slept on the floor on a Japanese mat. For fun, I let horses throw and stomp me. I wore jeans and jean jackets and pursued anorexia. I could never get myself thin enough for sex. My life was expanding away from me at unprecedented levels. I was intimate with constellations of gum spit out onto sidewalks. The Big Dipper seemed far too simplistic to admire.

I went to Israel and prayed at King David's tomb. I hoed weeds in the fields below the mount where Jesus gave the *Sermon on the Mount*. I drank Arab cough syrup flush with codeine. My best friend was a heroin addict. This was in the old days of heroin. Now heroin grows on pine trees in Vermont. I am trying to make sense of my life, but there is no reasonable narrative arc on which to hang it.

Belonging to clubs gives one prestige. I am a member of no club. That is why I will never be successful. I have lived in St. Augustine, Florida and New Orleans, Louisiana, both anachronistic locales. I pissed off all the used booksellers in both those towns—I don't know why. I alienated the woman who was giving me shelter merely by *thinking* that she was an alcoholic—she read my mind and was offended. Of course she was an alcoholic—who else would give me shelter? Her couch smelled like dead, lesbian animals. That was before lesbianism was acceptable.
I found out that my best friend had died of brain cancer and, as a result, almost ran over a black prostitute. That lady was a distant relative of mine.

My name is spelled Grabois, hers is Gravois. She lived in a house located under a freeway overpass—it felt very sheltered. After the near accident, she did my laundry at her dry-cleaning shop for free. She told me that she was glad she was black because she wouldn't want to be a victim of anti-Semitism. I told her that I was glad for her. We drank absinthe that her great-grandfather had saved for a special occasion.

Smokers

Smoking damages the tissues in your penis, but Viagra makes it all right, like Jesus died for your sins. You can sin and then repent, make it work in God's eyes. You can take the little blue pill, you can bring a woman to orgasm, and afterwards lay propped up in bed enjoying a cigarette together. You'll never see her again. She'll never see you again.

Smoking damages a lot of body parts. The airplane doesn't allow it. You can't disable the sensor in the toilet. The flight attendant watches you as if she knows that smoking is your healthiest vice. She is fresh from martial arts training. She knows how to control people in tight spaces, how to neutralize their bad intentions. She itches to try out her new skills. You live in a small space in a large world.

My rental car doesn't allow smoking. I open all the windows to the hot desert air. The tip of my cigarette is no hotter. For the first time in weeks I relax

J. Robert Oppenheimer was a smoker too. We also shared the *genius* designation. He died, aged sixty, after smoking four packs of unfiltered Chesterfields a day all his life, from the time he was five years old. He was a prodigy in so many ways. He built THE BOMB, then got blacklisted for being a commie.

No matter how good you are, no matter how bad, they'll get you. Like Dylan said: *Everybody must get stoned.* He also said: *It may be the devil or it may be the Lord, but you're gonna have to serve somebody.*

I serve ice cream to children. It's my job. Even with my PhD, it was the best I could get. The world recognized Oppenheimer's genius. It does not recognize mine. It doesn't bother me anymore. I'd rather serve children than the Devil or the Lord.

Ali

Muhammad Ali is in a coma. There is no parking in Flagstaff, Arizona, no parking garages, no parking meters. He started as Clay. I tried to diet. Instead I fattened on Nutella. Clay was his slave name. *Nurse Jackie* took an opioid on her one-year anniversary of sobriety. No Viet Cong ever called Muhammad Ali *nigger*.

I use miniature notepads to chart my progress as a human being. "Ali" is more than vanity. Ho Ho *Ho Chi Minh, NLF is gonna win.* My novel is now ranked just over 1.4 million on Amazon. I have to admit that it sucks, but it was the best I could do. Friends tell me they bought it, but that's the last I ever hear from them.

In Flagstaff, you must stay in your car and circle forever. It is worse than New York City. Nurse Jackie suffered a heroin overdose, and was rushed to Bellevue Hospital, where she had been hired and planned to resuscitate her career. I hear that the weather in Flagstaff is ideal. I hear that it is considered an ideal retirement destination by former members of the *National Liberation Front.*

George Foreman is still selling hamburger cookers. Some of my best friends are lesbians. I fantasize that I am making love to them. Sonny Liston was a friend of mine. Muhammad Ali has passed away.

Jewess

Whether you like them, or whether you're an anti-Semite, even if you fantasize whips and chains in Hitler's bunker with a beautiful lieutenant, you're all becoming Jews and Jewesses. You hide in dim rooms, the shine of the laptop on your face, studying words, manipulating them, as if in these words are wisdom and beauty. You wax eloquent over the process of Creation, and yes, you're pretentious, but you feel as if you're really getting somewhere.

You're a Jew or Jewess, but it's not God you glorify, only yourself. I'm not judging. What does it matter? Everyone knows God is an illusion, a human-created artifact. All is folly. Only some folly is more foolish than others.

You're a Jew or Jewess, because you stare at your screen instead of going outside to plant apple seeds like Johnny Appleseed, who ambled thousands of miles through the countryside. All these useless words. You're a member of a conquered people, an American. The wealthy haggle over your soul. You're a Jew or Jewess. You live in a pod of your own making. You're a Jew or Jewess. You've become one. You've been made one by the futility of your lives, your inability to make a difference.

You've become a Jew or Jewess. Me, I've always been one. So has Angela.

Angela goes to a tattoo parlor to get a prison camp number tattooed on her forearm, the same number her grandfather had in Auschwitz. The tattoo artist offers to do it for free. *I wish I could do this without needles,* he says. *I wish I didn't have to inflict pain, but it's a necessity of my career, just like it was necessary for the Nazis who were merely following orders. If the Holocaust happened at all, and wasn't just a figment of the Jewish imagination.*

Angela pulls her arm away. The buzzing needle hangs in the air. How had she begun this spiritual act by stumbling into the lair of this creep? A friend had recommended him. Sometimes you can't depend on friends.

Sometimes there's no one you can depend on.

Angela returns home. Her lover has been expecting her. He gently takes her wrist. *Where's the tattoo*, he asks.

There is no tattoo.

He kisses her forearm anyway.

Mitchell Krockmalnik Grabois has had over thirteen-hundred of his poems and fictions appear in literary magazines in the U.S. and abroad. He has been nominated for the Pushcart Prize (several times), The Best of the Net, and Best Small Fictions. He was awarded the 2017 Booranga Writers' Centre (Australia) Prize for Fiction. His novel, *Two-Headed Dog*, based on his work as a clinical psychologist in a state hospital, is available for Kindle and Nook, or as a print edition. He lives in Denver, Colorado, USA.

To read more of his work, Google: Mitchell Krockmalnik Grabois.

(Holy crap, this guy's good.)

Richard Rose

Three Stops on Route 15

(i)

Not just the sunken roof
but waviness of siding–
the tilted porch–
are signs that ownership has changed.
Freeloaders skitter down the walls.
Investment bankers calculate
their pull-out to the day and hour
from the high-rise to be built
for vacancy.
Deer visit in the afternoon,
passing through the rooms
as if the floors were marble
or a meadow.

(ii)

Simon Kenton left these parts
because he'd killed a man.
He went West with Clark,
fought Indians
and secretly returned,
discovering the man he'd killed
living with her
they'd fought over.
He went back West.
Delay had meant
he couldn't bring himself to mind.

Catharpin–
a name pronounced
more like cat harping
than cathartic;
a name chosen
for distinction:
nautical, the line
that holds the shroud–
names both creek and village.
Outsiders say it wrong.
Inland, nautical
only in the way hogsheads once were–
London-bound from river's edge–
Its Postmaster chose the name.
He could have named it for himself
but wanted no more rising from it
than he could live with.
To close the spread from *be* to *seem*
is beam enough from any eye.

Richard L. Rose taught and administered science programs for 35 years and wrote and composed for fifty years. His most recent opera productions are *The Fisher of the James* (2012), and the Capitol Opera Richmond productions of *La Rinuncia* and the *Missa brevis* in 2015 and *Monte & Pinky* in 2018. *Frameshifts* (2011) is his two-volume book of stories and poems; *Coming Around*, a companion work to the opera *Monte and Pinky*, was published in 2018 by Brandy Lane Press.

Visit him online at: https://frameshifts.com/

Caitlin Thomson

Scheduled Exodus

Your mother calls you, her voice caught
somewhere below a shriek and above
a scream. When you left the house this morning
you were wearing a blue shirt that I ironed,
the back still wrinkled a little. She tells you
that I am gone. That our drawers
no longer contain my clothes.

That Emily and Roberta's closets are cleaned
of everything but cobwebs. Her voice shakes,
tears gather in her eyes, I try to take her hand
but she brushes me off. I hear your shouts
on the other end of the line. Anger passes
through me in waves, but I am the beach today,
all of that sand that is pummeled against, over and

over, and does not react for centuries.
You ask where I could be and she says
we might be in Orlando. There was something
about Sea World scrawled on the calendar,
half erased. *Didn't Maria have friends there?*
your mother asks. *She used to*, you reply,
and go on to book plane tickets,

roaring on the other end of the line.
In twenty minutes the children are buckled
into their car seats, the car contains
all the seeds of our new life in the east.

Sacramento

To go missing from oneself, the type of curse reserved
for fairy tales. My aunt at forty-five is absent at this table.

She has to be reminded again about dinner. She knows what
hunger is, may never forget that, but she is always neglecting

something. Although so am I, come to think of it, the recycling growing in the bin. The appropriate word often alludes me.

We try patience as she hunts for our names in her memory, grows angry in the attempt. Confused by this child or that, her great nieces, two years ago she traveled miles for them, now she does not know them from any other child. I wonder if she knows that she has lost herself, though maybe she hasn't yet.

Caitlin Thomson has an MFA from Sarah Lawrence College. Her work has appeared in numerous anthologies and literary journals including: *The Adroit Journal, Rust + Moth, Barrow Street Journal,* and *The Pittsburgh Poetry Review.*

Visit her online at: www.caitlinthomson.com.

James F. Gaines

Unvoiced

As I speak to you I am
Just myself
When I call to you
I am not a mockingbird
Who does sing quite well
Don't get me wrong, but
I'm not trying to imitate
Mockingbird sings only bits of others'
Selves as the elders say he alone
When hummingbird's tobacco magic
Saved all existence
Did not voice his own joy
Borrowing from all the bird kin
It's not that I lack ear or talent
For when I call cardinal or barred owl
In their own music they call back
I do as I choose as
Right now I choose me
For I esteem your understanding
The notes of who I am
If you slept in the viburnum thicket
If your eyes revolved to the back of your head
If you were born on the isle of Terceira
I might feel the need
Temporarily to transform
But now is now
So like Popeye the Sailor
I'll toot my own little horn
Sooty as it may be

Tombs

When I was a grave digger
That windy summer on the North Shore
We carefully trimmed around tombstones
That scaled off like bits of desiccated skin

The oldest had a skull with dainty wings
And dates that begun with one and six
The skulls all seemed too surprised
To bother being sinister
Yet the burial ground near Danversport
Was filled with names of witches
No wonder they seemed overwhelmed
At the first glimpse of eternity
And then there were the orthodox Jews
Crammed thick and upright
Around a mysterious chapel
So little room left we often dug by hand
Wielding sharp spades and closely packing earth
That Bobby the Gloucester fisherman covered with a carpet
Cracking jokes about burying the non-believers
To keep his own spooked mind off an Azorean sorceress
Who'd predicted his death if he ever sailed again
When the first bereaved arrived
We'd don our yarmulkes to watch respectfully
While the rabbi chanted words
Already old two thousand years ago
And when the last mourners trailed away
We filled in slow with thick packed shovels
Building a grave that wouldn't subside
And then even if weeds still remained to mow
We'd work no more in or on the soil
Cleaning the dust off all our digging tools
The sundown deadline for the rituals was worth
Respect from us final carers for the passed

This Strange Adherence

Wet leaves
Clinging
To each other
This ephemeral touch
Lonely people
Clinging to each
Other
It does not last
The sun comes out

Drying up the bond
The wind rises
Separating leaves
The truth comes out
Drying up the bond
Necessity rises
Separating lovers
It is as nature
Makes it to be

Tewksbury

I can't for any price remember much
Just how we came to trading punch for punch;
Was it my name that smelled of doggie food
Or yours that rhymed conveniently with puke?
At any rate we banged around the locker room,
Aiming for pain while dodging spiky hooks,
Until the lad named Squeegee broke us up,
Moralizing us to pledge a grudging shake.
Then afterwards, your pitcher's letter stitched,
I wondered if you'd made the Show at last.
Some classmates told me you'd made quite a pile,
Then lost it all or cashed out – all the same,
Retired to the outer suburb ring,
Left voiceless on the board but mortgage-free,
That you misused a wife or two or three,
Or was it they who maybe misused you?
I know how women are, believe you me,
As hard to hold as the beads of mercury
You rolled around your palm in old Chem One,
Back in the moments that our rivalry
Boiled at the center of a clashing world.

James F. Gaines has been living on borrowed time for the past twenty years, thanks to a clever surgeon, and like all Americans, aims to keep on borrowing, since the universe has a lot of time to lend. His poetry has recently appeared in *El Portal*, *Red River Review*, *Avocet*, and other journals and his first collection, *Downriver Waltz*, will soon be available on Amazon. With his son John, he writes the science fiction *Forlani Saga* as J. M. R. Gaines; their first volume, *Life Sentence*, was published in 2016 and the sequel, *Spy Station*, was released last fall. They invite you to visit their blog, gainesscifi.blogspot.com.

Etta Johnson

The Mysterious Time Anagram

The hazy skies, the seagulls' cries, the grayish waves crashing on the shore, all seemed muted as if in a dream. I walked the beach close to the surf, the sand wet and cool between my toes. Nothing was real, nothing was clear. I was the sole human in the universe. The day did not become brighter, nor did it become darker, the crashing surf never ceased, and neither did the periodic predator-prey drama. As ghost crabs darted out of their sandy burrows, shore birds wheeled overhead and landing swooped up their dinner.

I walked on and on and on along the endless shoreline.

And suddenly there was no more. An immense rocky cliff blocked the beach. I couldn't see around it or over its great height. There was no way to wade around it since the waves dashed high, brutally battering the jagged rocks. I sat down on sand that was no longer warm, to get my bearings. I shivered as the wind whipped around the stone outcropping, and just as quickly the cloudy haze turned to dusk.

Now there was no visible light, only darkness, wind and salt-spray.

Two hundred years ago, the Collector had gathered grandfather clocks and gentlemen's pocket watches. A century ago it was clocks, watches and calendars of all kinds from villages, towns and cities. Today's haul included not only every variety of analog and digital watch and clock, personal diary and Day-timer, but a huge selection of electronics from tiny cell-phones to huge HD-TV screens, leaving homes, office buildings, malls and purses bare. Collecting every TIME measurement device aboard planet Earth was indeed an onerous task.

The red letters on the bus sign at the front of the vehicle rearranged themselves with four sharp ticks. The glowing red letters which had read TIME now said ITEM. The blurry vehicle moved swiftly, somehow inexorably through the darkness, targeting each stop accurately. The Collector jumped out, finding and piling items and storing them neatly in the vehicle's vast cargo-space.

Otherwise unremarkable in appearance, the Collector was clothed rather skimpily for the high, rare atmosphere in which he traveled. Neither old nor young, not clearly male or female, neither human nor creature of ancient myth or modern superhero, it was surrounded by short, swirling bursts of spectrum colors. Each foray into a building – cottage or high-rise, church or supermarket resulted in numerous time-related items amid the rainbow glow.

Perhaps more closely related to Santa Claus or Oz than to Apollo, Ra or Manco Capac, the COLLECTOR never swerved from his mission. Although he could collect every time item once annually, he couldn't stop their rapid replacement or proliferation. Nor did the Collector have the ultimate power over time. He was no Hercules to grasp the Earth and halt its revolution around the Sun. He could not keep the Earth still by clasping its axis pole, while holding tight to its equator belt. Unlike Santa, the Gift Giver, the Collector was just the item gleaner removing Time gadgets.

Suddenly the vehicle's glowing red letters ticked again, transposing into MITE. Simultaneously the vehicle dumped its gigantic cargo in an explosion of sound and light as tons of man-made products fell from the vehicle into an open crater. With one sucking motion like a mouth around a straw, the edges of the crater closed together. Only a small speck, a mite marred the land.

From my secluded post beside the rocks on the beach, I observed the awe-inspiring spectacle unfold.

But the vehicle, the bottomless vehicle was nowhere in sight. Had it simply dissipated into thin air along with its inexhaustible driver? Or had it too fallen into the crater, to be fossilized over the centuries?

Then a strange rainbow light twisted and turned against the dark sky until the letters EMIT emerged fully formed. I was as puzzled as to the meaning, as I was sure of its message. EMIT an anagram of TIME. Emit light, of course. Words, letters indubitably, meaning invariably intertwined.

As I strolled back along the beach, I pondered what I had seen. Was it a vision? A waking dream? An unusual atmospheric disturbance? A subconscious message? The inevitable result of my obsession with time? Perhaps only time would tell. Perhaps only time would solve the mystery of the time anagram.

Time Metaphors

I've thought and tried to puzzle out
The meaning of time metaphors.
I understand time science well,
But to me metaphors are literal.

Does life begin like a fairy tale?
A birth announcement sent to all:
"*Once upon a time* our baby came,
And lived happily ever after just the same."

I tried to *save time*, but had no PIN
No account to deposit savings in.
I dropped it in a piggy bank,
But there was not one coin to clank.

"*Take your time*!" she said quietly.
My pockets are full and my bag is too.
"Where should I take it?" I had to ask.
"Should I take it home so it will last?"

If I *kill time*, what will happen to me?
Will it be prison immediately?
Will the charge be 'murder with intent'?
Or will time become my best defense?

I recently had a bad accident,
But no emergency room for me.
I know that *time heals all wounds*,
So I'll just wait and see.

I wonder what happens when *time flies*. . .
Where's the scheduled arrival gate?
Must I hasten not to miss the flight,
Since I'm aware of being late?

I must make a quick decision
In which bin to put *wasted time*.
The trash truck will be coming soon,
But recycling's an ecological boon.

In the current *race against time*
The winner is unclear
Is it the beginning or the end
Of a month, day or year?

If *time is money,*
What's the rate of exchange?
Is it dollars or Euros?
What's the total range?

Time metaphors intrigue me
As I gaze upon the sea -
If *time and tide wait for no man,*
Will I, woman be surf-free?

Etta Johnson, teacher, artist, writer as well as family matriarch has long
created works of fact and fiction, poetry and prose, fabric art and collage
related to the endlessly fascinating topic of *time.*

Visit her online at: http://www.sites.google.com/site/content4ells
Linkedin: ejettajohns@gmail.com
e-book, Amazon, BN – *Please, Don't Call Me a Refugee*

Michael Garrigan

Beige Carpet Stuck Between Toes

gnarled spruce arch their backs
streaming thin branches across windows
blunted by sun stained taupe tapestries.

I never knew what towel to use
or when to unlace my shoes
before the carpet the TV the Sega
Sonic and X-men cartoons.

People Magazine headlines blurred
across a knee-high table, kitchen shadows
sipping cold tea all day, a full ashtray
of talk-show game-show chatter

breathe clouding stars
I wake up to a wet sleeping bag
afraid of spiders, afraid of eyes open to me
your screen door only inches away
I wanted to roll across
        the living room
                into the kitchen
to a bowl of Fruit Loops and a cup of orange juice
to drink the acidic fruity milky mix drowning in the spoon

the hedges a fort
kept close dreams
warm at the bottom of the bag
piles of acorns in mulch
for battle, a flashlight standing sentinel

I go camping
to feel the sun
nudge

my head
as birds flit
from branch to branch
over soft smoke of a doused fire pit.

A Bell

Kneeling at the altar,
a bell ring
Fills the empty church
pushing flickering light of prayer
candles into my periphery.

Father Joe shuffles out of the sacristy,
"That was God...", winks, tilts his head in a "now-you-know" way.
I continue my "Our Father" confident someone is listening,
ignoring the scratch of the Victorian red carpet against knees.

I haven't heard another bell since.

This upset me for years
until I realized that a bell
is not the only sound,
a robe does not make a priest,
an altar is not always carpeted.

Dead Salmon

I saw a photo of a dead salmon,
beautiful, spent, its dark red merging into the gray rock,
the stream licking at its tail,
his one eye, looking up at the sky, facing upstream.

I want to look like that when I pass -
as if I've used all the fat and blood
to end where I knew I needed to be
in order to complete the cycle.

Resting on a bed of moss and pine needles,
ferns growing through fingers spread upstream

reaching for the next bend, yet knowing that
it's ok not to reach it. Happy just dangling in the water.

Snotty Bacon

My grandpa started a fire
each morning when camping
before anyone else was up.

Steam vapors rise from a Florida storm,
cutting the world off at the knees,
leave slimy glimpses of worms wiggling on macadam.

He held my hand and told me they were sticks.
But they're moving. Nah, just sticks

Strokes took most of his speech, but not his humor.

Shaved head, staples a course crescent
moon groove across scalp,
tense shaking finger pointing
He'd stutter, "bu...bu...but I don't have a brain."
when someone would yell for hitting into them on the golf course.

> Deep, guttural laughing at obscene pain and fear of worms and
> tumors,
> Snotty bacon smoked in the steam of crackling twigs on cast iron
> Slick fat stopping abruptly at crispy edges.
> Early morning campfires before a day of fishing with twigs
> plucked off the road after a midday rain.

34

Dark gravel at five a.m.
covered by a hatch
of sleet and snow.

Empty parking lot.
Rhododendron leans in,
a rainbow trout on a hare's ear nymph.

Working downstream
Bridge to bridge.
Strip, strip, nudge and cast.

Trains lumber through -
freight, oil tankers, passenger cars -
serrated teethy cleaves and glinting sunlight of limestone and shale.

A grove of mid-century rust belt ranchers,
white porches splayed with rock salt slush,
ease their end into the valley, the river.

A ferruginous notch slices a path
in the eddies of the Appalachian plateau
like sycamore roots veined in snow.

Michael Garrigan lives along the Susquehanna River in Pennsylvania where he writes, teaches, and explores the river's tributaries with a fly rod. His essays and poems have appeared in *Gray's Sporting Journal, The Drake Magazine, Susquehanna Life Magazine,* and *San Pedro River Review.* He is currently working on a collection of poems.

Visit him online at: www.raftmanspath.com

Richard Luftig

Solstice

He thinks the best way
to deal with winter

is simply by staying
alive. It is the same

as how he puts up
with every day

loss; water a plant,
feed the distant cat.

His life is now a play
that people no longer

attend; much like
how the angled

light gets short
shrift this shortest

day of the year.
But still he will

follow the walkway
down to the bottom,

check the empty mailbox
that on the best of days

might be stuffed with circulars
that could fill at least part

of his afternoon,
the black ice of his drive

an overcoat he would
just as soon slip on.

True North

An Alberta wind is racing
the moon tonight, down
through the frozen fields
of flat, plain states. These

are the places I should know
by heart but can't quite remember.
I am searching again, behind
trees, under stones, for lost poems

that might write themselves
if only I would be still for a while,
keep silent, stay in one place

long enough to allow them in.
I take the compass from my pocket,
the one you pressed in my hand
the night I left, said how easily

I could find you if only I would
let the needle point true north,
put one foot ahead of the other,
until I made my way home.

Bach's Lunch

Twenty mouths to feed. It is a wonder how
Anna Magdalena could manage to send
her husband out with even a bit of schnitzel,
a mere taste of wurst wrapped in brown paper,
perhaps a few pfennigs for a draught of beer.

And he driven to distraction, twenty long years
in his duties to the city: tuning endlessly
recalcitrant organs, giving lessons,
teaching Latin, conducting boy-choirs
of balky sopranos looking forward
to the day their voices dropped and they
could get on with the rest of their lives.

Writing the weekly church cantata
with some critic always finding fault.
But *genug*, he decided one gray, Leipzig day.
Enough. He must compose for himself:
Masses, fugues, concertos,
counterpoints of angels dancing.
No, he would devote whatever time
he had left to the glory of God,
go wherever the music took, give it
everything he had and go for baroque.

Senior Center

We return day after day like migratory doves
to newspapers, books, the blue light of CNN,
the mute on. No, the local news is more important;
A friend's scheduled surgery, another remarrying
at age 83 to a babe ten years younger than himself.

Coffee and donuts, twenty-five cents each
from the bakery uptown, sprinkled with jokes
we've told dozens of times before.

Lunch; turkey a-la-king, Friday fish
for Catholics who swear they've never heard
of Vatican II. And the seating: always unreserved
which we've nevertheless been reserving for years.

Then the tables cleared for our games of canasta
that have gone on longer than forever: four-handed
if you don't count the folks commenting on each trick,
none of us ever trying for trump but rather
content to simply lay down our hearts.

Cemetery

The only mourners left;
these summer storms
those winter moons.

Winds that sand
away the names
on tombstones

to flatness as if
no one ever lived
here to farm the fields.

And someday,
when even the dead
are not looking,

the centurion pines
standing guard
nearby will split,

splinter, collapse,
from lightening
or ice-laden limbs

like everything else
in these plains,
years before their time.

Richard Luftig is a professor emeritus of educational psychology and special education at Miami University in Ohio who now resides in California. He is a recipient of the Cincinnati Post-Corbett Foundation Award for Literature. His poems and short stories have appeared in numerous literary journals in the United States and internationally in Europe, Asia and Australia. His work has been submitted for the Pushcart Prize.

Sarah Snyder

A Matter of Life

The sign in the airplane lavatory,
"As a Courtesy to the Next Passenger
You May Wipe the Sink off
with Your Paper Towel"

makes me want to write
a poem. I'll call it "Might be a Sign."
I think about pulling out my lipstick,
starting the first draft on the mirror,

Thinking of washing gods,
but don't, open the flimsy, folding door,
move through the chambered plane,
to my slotted seat, the time for washing past,

let the sound of water settle into clouds
and touch the ring of gold and diamonds
my mother used to wear on a hand that knew
the archeology of kneading,

the click clack of needles,
knitting a sock or sweater from skeins,
the hiss of steam as she pressed hard
to unwrinkle the cotton of cuffs and sheets.

The diamonds glint in a sun
framed by the small window—
and outside—an engine's violet flame,
and below, parceled land.

To a Fragile Piece

The squirrel who digs in the flower bed and scurries
up the wooden steps almost to the sliding glass door
might be my mother or father.

My mother's metal sifter making small clouds
of flour, those battered shallow pans, an apron
tied haphazardly around her waist.

My father finding the trowel for burying
the faceted coal chunk I'd pocketed
from the black pile toppling onto Second Street.

And what remains
underground—a diamond,
the distance in the rush over falls.

A Shattered Skiff

I saw one once, heaved onto the sand,
covered in kelp—a broken boat,
a broken story in an unbroken
circle of what lands at our feet,

in our hands. The story of families
fleeing the rooflines they know

to seek unfettered light
in a different realm, watch

it move into the smallest things—
inlets, needled trees, on every facet

of the sea beyond a suddenness
of banked clouds.

Whitewater Rafting on the Naranjo River in Costa Rica

Launched from the boat
into airless, sharpened water—

death seemed to swing open
under a churning river crowded

with boulders until sky replaced
that long quiet, our guide wrenching me

into the thick rubber boat
choking. For days and days

I'd be in this marrow—airborne…
under…lifted—as if this sequence

were stored in each cell
unwilling to surrender.

Viewpoint

Martial law was his greatest work,
thought the general in his crisp,
khaki uniform. This was his country,
his Myanmar. All of his underlings

in green caps following.
I can see my son
riding on the back
of a dilapidated motorcycle,

thankfully covered in cloth and dust.
But the general didn't see him,
did not see the work he was doing
at the orphanage, trekking up mountains,

leading others to Buddhist temples
in this lush land. Did not see
the tattoo below the layers
of sweaty clothes—

a peacock,
the symbol of opposition
moving across
the country.

Sarah Dickenson Snyder has written poetry since she knew there was a form with conscious line breaks. She has two poetry collections, *The Human Contract* and *Notes from a Nomad*. Recently, her work has in *Stirring: A Literary Journal, Whale Road Review, Front Porch, The Sewanee Review,* and *RHINO.* In 2016, she was a 30/30 Poet for Tupelo Press. One poem was selected by Mass Poetry Festival Migration Contest to be stenciled on the sidewalk in Salem for the 2017 festival. Another was nominated for Best of Net 2017.

Visit her online at: www.sarahdickensonsnyder.com

Ben Sloan

Ballpoint Pen

"You write like a girl,"
a student told me
which I realize now
is a high compliment,
prompting me to want to
thank you Mrs. Airsman,
my short, stout, brisk
first grade teacher
whose classroom was
encircled, as if by a belt,
by pairs of capital and
lowercase cursive letters
I practiced stringing
together with a pen
tightly spooled inside
of which I discovered
every obscene word
I had ever heard.
To this day I much prefer
the spring-loaded
push button model
patented in 1888,
the same year
Harpo Marx was born,
who, like the ballpoint pen,
is rumored to have been mute
but we all know was not.

School Crosswalk Sign

He leans above her, his arm, if he
had arms, reaching, if he could reach,
to assist her in crossing the street, if they
could cross the street, but of course they
never will because they have no eyes,

no faces, only round blank black balls
for heads. And perhaps the saddest part
is they have neither hands nor feet,
are firmly planted, screwed fast against
a tall metal pole, itself jammed deep into

the earth, much like Christ in this regard.
But despite their hardships, despite their many
sorrows, they continue to sing a chartreuse
caution song for all who pass. But this singing
is not so much eternal as permanent.

The Birth of Charles Baudelaire

Nature counts on people being confused.
For example he asks does she love me
or was it that she just wanted to use
me for sex? Of course nobody can be
sure of the answer, most of all the two
of them. Leaning on the fence to confer,
neighbors have taken sides on the issue.
These over here insist that he loves her,
but those over there say she only wants
to do what's needed to get in his pants.
But nobody cares really who has won.
The only point is that the deed was done.
Next door is a cute but screaming baby.
That is all nature cares about, really.

Table Mountain Pine
for Ian

As my 17-year-old son goes to the car
to drive somewhere to find a tree to draw
as his art class homework assignment
I realize I might never see him again.
On prom night when his friend and
his friend's father knocked one night
and took me out to their van and opened

the side door, he was strapped in
safe but completely limp, looking dead,
but having been through all this once before
with his older sister, I knew he was just dead
drunk. Today I knew I had to say something to him,
so as he put his easel in the back end I said,
Whatever you do remember one important thing:
Some trees are more cooperative than others.

Toothpaste

This machine I just invented
will pluck a dead buffalo

out from between the sun's teeth,
reupholstering her bleached bones

so she can once again be seen nibbling
along the grassy margins of Nebraska.

You can see an entire Indian nation returning
to the western plains if you look in my eyes.

I have brought it to show to you today
because it will return to our mouths

those words we said to one another.
It will also put toothpaste back into its tube.

Growing up in rural southeast Missouri, Ben Sloan studied at Brooklyn
College and the CUNY Graduate Center. His poems have appeared in the
Hamilton Stone Review, *Off the Coast*, the *Hartskill Review*, the *Ozone Park Journal*,
the *Saint Ann's Review*, *Straylight*, and *Third Wednesday*. Living now in
Charlottesville, he teaches at Piedmont Virginia Community College, the
Fluvanna Correctional Center for Women, and the Buckingham Correctional
Center.

Brielle Perry

Lost Letters

On the first day of kindergarten
I wrote the letter "B" on my name tag
And nothing else
"B" for Brielle
Because "B" reminded me of balloons
"B" stood for bubbles, bowties, butterflies,
"B" for baboon, "B" for banana
Alphabet picture books had taught me everything I needed to know
About the letter "B"
"B" stood for blossom
So I wrote the letter "B"
On my name tag
And nothing else

But Kindergarten passed
Then it was first grade, third grade, sixth grade, ninth grade,
"B" started to become… boring
"B" seemed to bother people
They told me "B" meant bitter
It was brought to my attention
That "B" was the second letter of the alphabet
Never the first, never the best, never quite good enough
"B" led to bullying
"B" made me below-average
I had to ask myself
Since when did "B" stand for broken?
If "B" was my identity,
Did that mean I was burdened, and beaten, and always the one to blame?
My blossom had been blown to bits
And I was begging for "B" to mean
Ballerina or basketball or birthday cake
The way it once did
And I kept believing that I was battered and bent
Until I met you

A stranger on the street
I remember wearing the letter "B" on a name tag

And nothing else

You looked at it and said
"B"?
"B" as in... brave?
"B" as in brilliant?
"B" as in bold, "B" for bright, "B" meaning beyond in all the best ways?
Wait, no...
 "B" for beautiful?

Shock fell over me
It was bizarre that a stranger
Could change what I had been contemplating for years
In just a single moment
When you looked at "B" with a better point of view
You made me realize
That maybe "B" wasn't so bad after all
Maybe I wasn't so bad after all

So I smiled, and nodded.
"Yes," I replied.
"B" for Brielle.

How to Go from Super Nerd to Super Model in Just Three Days

It began like any other snack time. The teenagers split up into their usual cliques, because puberty and insecurity seem to go hand in hand. And, of course, being the outcast because of my glasses, and braces, and oversized nose and fear of socialization and all-things-typical-nerd, I was sitting alone. In the back corner. Reading a comic book and eating a pack of Craisins. *What a stud.*

I had kind of given up on the whole "normal thing" a long time ago. It had only taken a few days at my new high school to realize that nobody wanted to be around me, the one and only Eugene Wartmeyer. It was probably because of the little things, like the way I stuttered, or the fact that I sometimes forgot to blink for uncomfortably long periods of time. I figured I would always be ordinarily unordinary because it was impossible to change destiny. And my gigantic nose. So, of course, I hadn't expected learning to drink with my pinkie up or practicing how to dance with my imaginary girlfriend at a teenage cotillion camp would lead to anything special. And I certainly wasn't going to find a bright future in that box of Craisins, or on the "kick me" sign that was probably taped to my back.

But as I was sitting there, immersed in the thrilling story of *Titan the Super Tortoise*, my Krusty Krab Pizza ringtone suddenly blared from my pocket. I froze. My face turned paler than my thighs. I could feel the heat radiating from about sixty other pairs of eyes as Spongebob continued to sing from my pants.

And then, I realized I couldn't match every single one of the awkward stares piercing a hole straight through my already delicate dignity, so I bolted to escape. I ran as fast as I could, which probably looked more like an elephant with a broken leg, but this moment represented life or death in the world of social statuses. Moments later, I burst through the extremely heavy ballroom doors and sprinted down the hallway until I came to a dead end. I stopped, exhausted, and let out a sigh of relief.

At this point, I had sweat all the way through my grey t-shirt, I was pretty close to having an asthma attack, and I had already missed the phone call. I combed my fingers through my choppy, Justin-Bieber-wannabe hair and tried to recover from the traumatizing experience. I leaned back and shivered as the frigid tile on the wall brushed the skin of my arms. The slippery texture sent me sliding down onto the carpet as I sat in the silence and closed my eyes. I didn't think returning to snack time would be a good idea. It wasn't like anyone was missing me anyway.

But then, while I was still recovering from my latest nerd-world problem, my pants rang again and I nearly jumped right out of them. My hand flew to my face in a violent spasm and knocked my thick-rimmed glasses to the ground. The incessant noise of the phone call was overwhelming and now I was blind and I felt like I was gonna cry. But I managed to keep it together. Kind of.

The ringing finally halted as my stubby finger pressed the talk button and accepted the call. I tried my best to collect myself. I cleared my throat and flipped my hair, proceeding to speak in a low, soothing, masculine voice, which was quite the opposite of my regular one. Maybe I could make a positive first impression for once.

"Hello."

"Good afternoon, I'm calling for Sammy Stevenson? I have some very special news."

The nasally voice belonged to a woman. I was thinking typical librarian secretary: ballerina bun, glasses on a chain, and an ugly pantsuit. This was weird. I wasn't used to girls calling me.

"Wait, what? I'm not Stevie... what was the last name again—"

"Sammy Stevenson. I'm calling because—"

"No, you can't have my credit card number," I blurted out. I smirked, clearly proud of myself for detecting the scam.

The lady paused for a long time. *Was it something I said?* I fidgeted

nervously as I waited for her response. When the silence
continued for more than ten seconds, I took a different approach. My defense
skills kicked in.

"My mom told me not to talk to strangers."

Again, no answer. I imagined her lips conforming into a thin line and
her venomous eyes glaring at me through the phone.

"Look, kid. I don't get paid enough to do this job. And I'm pretty
sure you aren't Sammy Stevenson. So, could you at least take a message?"

"Uh, sure," I responded as casually as I could. I waited. And waited.
And when she didn't say anything, I did the most logical thing I could think
of.

"At the tone, please record your message… when you have finished
recording, hang up or… well don't press one because there aren't any more
options… beeeeeep."

I was tremendously relieved when I heard her voice. "Good
afternoon, this is Chelsea Waters from the team that brings you America's
Next Top Model. I'm calling on behalf of Sammy Stevenson regarding an
audition for the show that took place last Thursday. We would like to
congratulate you with an invitation to attend a callback this Friday, June 17th,
at 3:00 pm. The competition is heating up, so don't miss your chance
to win the million-dollar cash prize! Please direct any further questions to
www.americanmodelstatus.com. Thank you for participating, and we hope to see
you soon!"

Her words were followed by a click as the other end of the line was
submerged in an eerie silence.

I scratched my head out of confusion and curiosity. I knew that I
wasn't Sammy Stevenson. I knew that I had never walked in high heels or
worn makeup before. But I also knew that I was willing to do just about
anything for a million dollars.

Brielle Perry, a passionate writer since the age of seven, has had poems and
stories featured across various mediums. Her work was recently published on
bullyingrecovery.org, a blog run by author, Alan Eisenberg. She was also the
2017 Burke TAB Winter Writing Contest runner-up as well as the school
winner of the NCTE Writing Competition, and her submissions went on to
represent Lake Braddock Secondary School at the national level. In addition,
she has been featured as a guest writer for *The Bear Facts,* her school's
newspaper. She has also competed twice in The Hyperbole, the largest youth
poetry slam in Virginia. Aside from writing, she appreciates running, art,
music, dogs, and really nice people.

Mary Kay Wulf

The Girl in Between

She saw it winking at her as soon as she arrived home. When Winnie opened the door and stepped into the short, dark hallway of her studio apartment, the button light flashed, yes, red. She had cleaned teeth all day — eight mouths total — in a fancy pants K Street dental office. The blinking answering machine offered a novelty or some variation after a day of tedium (hers) and torture (her patients'). Honestly, she wondered how much longer she could stand working in people's mouths. It was 1983. She'd moved to DC two years earlier to pursue a professional career in the theater, and all she'd done was black box stuff here and there for no pay. But the rent was due monthly and dental hygiene paid that and every other bill. In fact, her bread and butter job paid very well, but the boredom was sufficient to stoke thoughts of self-slaughter. As a profession, dentists had the highest rate of suicide, so it made sense that hygienists were right up there, too.

She read the counter: two calls. It meant someone had thought of her, perhaps someone wanted her for something: an audition, a part in a play, a date, anything. She tossed her sweater and purse on the king-size bed that took up a third of the studio. Like most of her furniture, the bed— a monster mattress atop a box spring standing high on boards and cinder blocks— had come with the illegal sublet. Sandy, the smiling PhD student who ripped her off on the rent, was well over six feet, and when he'd occupied the place, he hadn't cared that the giant bed was the first thing people saw when they entered. Winnie thought it sent the wrong message.

It was 5:50 on a Monday evening, the second week of April. The Panasonic *Easa-Phone* rested on a matching cinder block and plank wall unit opposite. She sat on the corner of the bed and hit PLAY. Her mackerel tabby leapt onto her lap and sank his teeth into her cheek when she tried to kiss him. As Winnie listened to the first of the two messages, her bowels heaved and the connection between her mind and body seemed to snap. Who in Christ did what? The message was a doozy. She hit REWIND, shook her head, and chanted *sotto voce*, "Oh shit, oh shit, oh shit…"

Normally, she loved all the new technology, that machine in particular. How had humankind managed to maintain relationships, especially romantic ones, before this invention? Sure, she had recently engaged in a more primitive form of communication with her new neighbor downstairs who worked at National Geographic Magazine. She'd started that odd ball rolling by tying a jokey, come hither note to a long piece of dental floss and lowering it down through the casement window of their shared bathroom well. She was so lonely, and he was so cute. After a few days of flirty up and down messages, she and Carl had a casual dinner in a neighborhood sushi joint. Dutch treat. Then he left town for a few days and returned with the gift of a necklace, a strand of miniature red and green clay peppers strung on a black silk cord, made, he said, by his mother in Albuquerque. Gee, she thought, he loves me, and they had sex on the carpet in the darkness of his unfurnished studio. And that was it. Without another word or note, he went back to being just another neighbor.

"DC is like that. I warned you when you moved here. It's a candy store for men," her sister told her. Lucy lived in the twin apartment building next door. She was younger than Winnie but had moved to Washington a few years earlier and was wiser to the ways of Washington males.

A month later, Winnie learned from the lady who lived under Carl, at the garden level of their building — the basement really — that he was engaged to a girl in another city. The creep.

Now she turned the volume to max on the Panasonic and listened a second time. Was it a joke? A variation of the actor's nightmare cooked up by one of her friends? Or an enemy? The voice was female and familiar. oh, so familiar.

"Winnie, this is Margaret from stage management. Alice Langford was admitted to the hospital today." Winnie's insides swam in adrenalin. She hit PAUSE and pondered. When people were admitted to a hospital, they usually weren't found on the professional stage the following day or were they? The theater was dark on Mondays, but on Tuesday—tomorrow— the show would resume for three more weeks of a six-week run. So, Miss Langford had gotten through the five-show weekend like the professional she was and then . . . what? Collapse from exhaustion? Heart attack? Overdose? With actors you never knew.

Winnie'd had her own troubles with booze. In those first two years in DC, she'd ruined a rash of auditions because she'd gotten too drunk the night before to learn her lines. She finally traded her weeknight six-pack of cheap beer and weekend vodkas for dark smoky rooms filled with recovering drunks who told great stories. Her sister's ultimatum and her own fumbling hands inside her patients' mouths helped decide things, too. What if she maimed a patient through negligence? She could lose her license and get slapped with a malpractice suit followed by a hefty fine or a jail sentence, whichever the court decided.

Winnie released the PAUSE button, and the nightmare resumed.

"You'll be going on in the role of Gertrude tomorrow night," said Margaret.

Winnie pressed PAUSE again. The bastards. How could they? Sure, she'd been told over and over as the sole female understudy that she'd probably go on for Misty, the girl who played Ophelia. The beautiful, young New York actress playing that part had been lured to Washington because her mother lay dying just over the Potomac in Virginia; it probably hadn't hurt that an iconic British film director was flown in from London to direct the show. Winnie had done as she was told and committed every line of Ophelia's to memory so they were trippingly on the tip of her tongue. She conjured and recited them daily, anywhere, at any moment: scrubbing instruments, developing X-rays, teaching her patients how to floss. She'd seen the production six times during and after previews, and she knew Ophelia's blocking by heart. But *Gertrude*? That old lady? Winnie recalled her Latin, *Omnia Vanitas*.

There was more. "Please call Beth in costumes as soon as you get this. They're waiting for you, Winnie. You'll have a fitting tonight as soon as you can get up here. Your rehearsal call for tomorrow morning is 9:00 AM on stage. We'll run through your scenes with as many actors as we can reach on short notice. Any questions, call me."

She snapped the OFF button and murmured, "Yes, I have a question, goddam it: Why Gertrude?"

The second message was from costumes. "Hi. This is Beth in costumes…"

"For Christ's sake," Winnie cried, "I'm just a dental hygienist who likes Shakespeare. Don't they understand that? You want a tragedy? Plug me into *Hamlet* and I'll hand you a tragedy." She fed the cat and called a cab. She aspired to be an actress but not like this. This was baleful. Better to coddle an improbable dream than have to perform on a professional stage in a big city and not know your lines. For years she'd tried to wrench the passion for acting out of her future. Why couldn't she be content cleaning teeth like every other dental hygienist she knew? Her dream of a life in the theater was nothing like this current manifestation; this was more like an abscessed tooth that bubbled and troubled and pained her to tears.

Before she left, Winnie called the dental office. It was after hours. Good, she thought. She'd get *their* machine. Some of her best acting had been opposite that machine. Whenever Winnie played sick, it was significantly more challenging to keep up the act when the receptionist picked up the phone and then passed it to the office manager. Interrogations by two angry ladies were tough on the nerves. But now, if they learned she was out all day Tuesday because she played Gertrude in *Hamlet* on the Hill Tuesday night, they might fire her. Too bad. It was a chance she had to take.

She left a halting, hoarse message saying that she'd developed a fever on the bus home, and she was so sorry, but she better not come into the office tomorrow in case she was contagious. In DC she cleaned the teeth of diplomats and judges, congressmen and journalists, whistleblowers and mercenaries. They didn't care if she was sick. They always booked three months ahead and knew she wore a mask. Her patients blew their stacks when their appointments were cancelled. And their abuse came down second-hand and hard on her. Some left the practice. She'd been warned by the front office about getting sick and staying home, and they always called midday to check up on her, to confirm she was in bed and then make her promise to come to work the following day. If she missed their call because she was out on an audition, she'd call back and lie twice and say she'd gone to the doctor. It was a cat and mouse thing she played whenever the theater beckoned.

Like an appendage, she carried it around wherever she went. Now she opened the rolled, stained, scribbled up paperback copy of the play. She had approximately half of Gertrude memorized. The rest of it, the second half, including the monologue describing Ophelia's death by drowning, was a blank and she had only 24 hours to learn it. Lucy — afflicted by a similar performance bug — was still at Catholic U, where she majored in voice, so Winnie slipped a note under her door. It read: *Guess who has to go on as Gertrude tomorrow night? Goddamn Gertrude! Help! Can you please, oh please, go over the lines with me tonight, dear sister?*

It was still daylight as she waited for the cab outside her building across the street from the Soviet embassy. She liked to watch the place for spies. The USSR in the '80's was shaky and espionage was popping; political barriers were crumbling in all sectors. Even the theaters were drunk on freedom. The best crop of European directors, East and West, Communist or not, were invited to the Equity houses in Washington. Liberated from censorship, they elegantly blew the top off traditional direction and engendered a similar spirit in the small, tight, waiver companies around the city. Winnie appreciated the scene and took part in it for no pay, but her heart was in the classics and making it big.

That evening she eschewed spying and confined her brain to the script. She wanted to weep, except she knew histrionics wouldn't help. Save them for the Queen, she told herself. The lustful queen. Hamlet's mother. Hamlet. Hank Brody was Hamlet, brought all the way from London by his mentor, an experimental film director, famous for his creative genius. Winnie shook at the thought of facing Hank. By all accounts, he was terrible and magnificent. Backstage, according to the American actors in the show, who were themselves, stellar, he was a volatile, nasty prick. He'd made it known how much he hated stooping to the level of regional theater in the US— in this case, a small house, a wooden three-tiered replica of an Elizabethan inn. Winnie supposed the bad chemistry had something to do with playing the part of Hamlet, too. He had to deliver all those lines and speeches that the public thought they knew: "Get thee to a nunnery," "To be or not to be,"

"Alas, poor Yorick! I knew him, Horatio." The audience waited and shifted in their seats to hear the famous words spoken with a British accent by a handsome, dark haired, brooding Irishman in a black doublet, matching britches, and hose. Winnie loved the black hose. Oh yes, the pressure on him to do what legions of great actors had done before him was tremendous, but he was brazen enough to pull it off with aplomb. The only thing missing as he sauntered downstage center to deliver his best speech was one raised middle finger to flip off the world.

One night he'd vented his fury on a gentleman in the front row who was reading the program when Hank began his, "To be or not to be" soliloquy. He paused after the first couplet, leaned down, and tore the magazine from man's grasp. Then he resumed the famous monologue while he ripped the pages apart and tossed the mess back to the offender's lap. He was erratic and cocky. It was rumored he kept a bottle in his dressing room and sipped between acts on the five show weekends. By Sunday night, he played high, wide, and fast with his heavy sword and dagger in the fight scenes. Other actors complained. His throat, he told management. Too bad, they'd said, and took his booze away. He just smuggled in more.

She slid into the cab and told her Ethiopian driver, "Capitol Hill, please, as quickly as you can." Cabs in the District were affordable. They charged by the number of zones the taxi crossed. In Winnie's case, she lived on the opposite side of town, but it was only three zones because she knew where to get out before the driver crossed into the fourth. They flew down Foxhall to Canal and ran along the Potomac. If Hank hated the actors he worked with now ... oh, boy, oh, boy, she sighed. She was younger than he and frightfully inexperienced, the real green girl, and now she had to play his mom. The cabdriver climbed the hill and dropped her off two blocks from the theater.

Her fitting was harried and complex. The corset and red velvet gown were two sizes too big. While three seamstresses pulled and pinned, she held her script and memorized. It was a mild comfort to know she wouldn't be the only one working late that night. She glanced at her reflection in the long mirror on the wall opposite and thought the décolletage was a bit daring. In every way she failed to fit the profile of a matron. They advised her to line her face when she applied makeup. She winced at the idea. Just another vain actress at heart, she hoped to look her best. For him. She was relieved to learn they hadn't time to fit her in a wig. Most period wigs looked like wigs if they weren't customized and made by a master. She was ashamed of herself and her dearth of professionalism. How could she aspire to a career on the stage with such conceit coursing through her nature? She ought to give up Shakespeare, she thought, and move to Hollywood and do car commercials. No, she wasn't pretty enough for those. But maybe Ajax or diapers. Yes, that would serve her right.

Winnie returned home to Glover Park and spent the remainder of the evening with Lucy in her studio apartment. Her sister was thrilled at the news and patiently fed Winnie lines and corrected her errors. They sat in the kitchenette.

"Even though he's dead, every single word counts in Shakespeare. I can't make even the tiniest mistake because it won't scan, so stop me if I do, okay?" Winnie insisted.

"Sure," said Lucy.

The girls trudged like turtles through the text. Cramming verse was thorny stuff. They employed tricks with images, melody, and rhythm to get the most complex sections of the text to stick. The cues were king—the queen's lines often a simple, earnest inversion, protestation, or emendation. King: "Thanks, Rosencrantz and gentle Guildenstern." Queen: "Thanks Guildenstern and gentle Rosencrantz." It was late and Lucy looked anxious.

"How am I doing?" Winnie asked her sister.

Lucy rose from the kitchen table for two and walked into the living/bedroom. Winnie thought she caught her sister in the act of rolling her eyes in the mirror over the pullout sofa.

"Great," Lucy said. "Really, just great." They worked until midnight. "Sleep might do you more good at this point," Lucy said. "How do you feel?"

"Pretty solid," Winnie said. She secretly wondered if she could sneak down to Union Station in the dark and hop on the Amtrak to anywhere. She walked to the door and kissed Lucy goodnight. "I have to do it, don't I?"

"Of course you have to do it." Her sister shivered under the porch light. "You dodo bird, this is what you wanted. It's an honor. Think of it like that. This is what they hired you for, and, hey, it could turn out to be your big break, Win."

"Oh, whatever happens it's gonna be big all right, but it won't be my break. The casting is all off," said Winnie. "They picked me for the job because I'm too old to play Ophelia and too young to play Gertrude. They saved money by hiring a girl in between. And who can blame them? That's the theater for you. I love you." They embraced and made their secret family victory sign.

"Don't forget to leave me a ticket at the box office. Call me at lunch tomorrow and tell me how it's going." Lucy had seen the show, and she, too, had a crush on Hank.

"Sure." Winnie sprinted across the wet grass and took the steps two at a time to her apartment. She washed her hair, packed her stage make-up, and set her alarm clock.

She tossed around on the giant bed. She *really* didn't want to play Gertrude. She didn't want to step in for Alice, who was over 40 and a company player. She wanted to be Misty, who at 26, was glamorous and on her way up. Misty had a pale peach complexion that she streaked with fresh mud for the mad scene. Her hair was long and red, with curls that resembled a mass of fine coils from a box-spring. She stuck sticks and leaves in the curls for her big scene. Winnie's hair, at 34, was shoulder length blond made brown by winter. Misty lived in New York and had recently starred in a period film with an international cast. In two weeks Winnie was scheduled to begin evening rehearsals for a tiny role in a new play produced by a maniac who mismanaged a 55-seat theater in a crumbling part of DC. But what really got Winnie was Misty's brilliance. She was in awe of Misty's talent. She wondered how the younger woman did it. Winnie wanted to play Misty. She wanted to *be* Misty. Winnie slept with the script under her pillow in case it was true that lines could be transferred and absorbed through feathers. She dreamed in blank verse and woke up with butterflies.

She recited aloud from the moment she opened her eyes to the time they buzzed her in through the heavy front doors of the theater. It was an unseasonably cold morning. The mood inside the dark house was somber, and it dawned on her that the situation from all angles was grave indeed. Though they weren't divulging any whys or wherefores, the concern over Alice Langford's health was uppermost in the minds of the staff. It didn't sound like life or death, and Winnie didn't probe. Alice was not her favorite person that day.

The stage manager approached her with an expression of anxiety and pity. "How are you on lines?" Margaret asked, wearing a crown of headphones.

"Not good. If you'd called me in for Ophelia like you promised…" Winnie blinked away tears.

A few months earlier Margaret had directed Winnie in a one-act for a festival of new plays on 14th Street. "You'll be fine."

"I don't have the muddy death speech in its entirety. We have to trim it, and I promise I'll know it all by tomorrow night."

"You can read it. Carry the script on."

"I can't. The script doesn't go with the costume. Please, let's just cut a few lines. No one will notice. And if they do, they'll chalk it up to terror. Mine."

The stage manager relented, and they made some internal cuts together.

Margaret's assistant took Winnie downstairs to the dressing room that Misty shared with Alice, and handed her the floor length rehearsal skirt hanging from the costume rack. Then the assistant told her to remain there until she was called.

Winnie flipped through her script and observed the structure of the role as she'd highlighted it in yellow. Apart from the entrances and exits, and the blocking and props, all for which the company would supply help, the part of the Queen was relatively small. Except for the closet scene with Hamlet and the monologue describing Ophelia's muddy death by drowning, it consisted of fairly short scenes. There seemed ample time to study the lines between each one. Winnie figured if she chopped the role into bite-size bits and crammed for them one at a time backstage just prior to going on, she might be able to do it. Yes, that was her best chance for success. When she thought of the role in its entirety, she wanted to throw up. Think only of what comes next, she told herself.

Margaret's booming voice called her to places over the intercom.

Some of the actors milled around the house. Winnie knew a few of them personally and all of them by sight. She sensed they were visibly rattled at the prospect of spending their day preparing for a potential disaster that night. And suddenly he was there, scowling. Hank, looking frankly miserable. Margaret rushed over to him. He was compact and perfectly made. His mad brown eyes were perfectly spaced, his nose was straight and strong, and his mouth, his lips, when he wasn't scowling which was never, were perfect for speechifying and perhaps even kissing. Margaret motioned for Winnie to join them. She approached with trepidation.

He looked at her and protested in his trained Richard Burton voice, "You're too young to play my mother." He turned and glared at Margaret. The other actors watched. Winnie had no answer. He turned back to her and asked how many times she'd seen the show.

"Six," she murmured. "And...and you, you're just so wonderful."

He set his jaw and strutted off to his dressing room.

The arduous task of plugging an understudy into Shakespeare's best began. Winnie loved the play and Hank in the play, and that got her through the morning. All the actors except Misty, who'd been excused for the purpose of spending the day with her mother, came and went as their scenes were scheduled. They were overtly sympathetic and helpful, including Hank on occasion. On the lunch break, she sat in the lobby, script in hand, and ate a chicken wing and an apple out of Tupperware. She faced the glass doors of the entrance, and when it started to snow, she mourned the death of the cherry blossoms that had bloomed early that year around the Jefferson Memorial. But she rejoiced, too, because she loved snow on Capitol Hill. All that white. The odd, unseasonable weather she took as a good omen.

By late afternoon she knelt over Ophelia's grave and spoke, "Sweets to the sweet. Farewell." Dizzy from all the direction, she paused and shook her head. "I...I can't remember anymore." The remainder of the speech, "I hoped thou shouldst have been my Hamlet's wife. I thought thy bride-bed to have deck'd, sweet maid, and not have strew'd thy grave," had not yet made its way off the page and into her head. She looked up at the actor playing Laertes.

"Michael, when I toss my bouquet of funeral flowers into the grave, can that be your cue for, 'O treble woe?' Can you take a visual cue? Just for tonight?"

"Of course," said Michael. A long-time company member, he'd always been kind to her.

They broke for dinner with nods of encouragement, but Winnie saw they were relieved it was she and not them who had to face the horror to come. She'd known and conquered terror in the theater before, in *this* theater, in fact, the previous season. Always the bridesmaid, she was understudying then, too, and a similar call had come. On that particular Sunday evening, she'd made her entrance upstage onto a Juliette balcony as Inés in Calderon's *The Mayor of Zalamea* and was struck dumb. It took three, perhaps even four beats and four actors looking up at her, waiting for her tongue to unlock itself. And once it did, she entered the world of the play and remained there until the curtain call, after which she was transported for weeks. Then, as now she was a little in love with the actor playing the lead. She'd had to embrace and kiss that one on the lips, too. Hank would not kiss her in this production except on her forehead or the hand as she lay dead after drinking from the poisoned cup. That would be nice enough.

She walked alone to a nearby café and bought a slice of cheese pizza and a pop to go. When she returned to the theater, a chrome stand stood in the lobby announcing her presence in the production in place of Alice Langford. Great, she thought, now the audience will know who to boo. She ate and studied in her cold dressing room. Then she laid out her towel on the table and unpacked her make-up. The only heat came from the naked light bulbs surrounding her mirror. The actors arrived with the cold on their coats. Most ducked their heads into her room and told her to break a leg. Some handed her cards with the same wish spelled out. Hank dropped a pretty postcard on her table addressed to the 'Lustful Queen' and signed, 'Love, Hank.' It was just what actors did.

Margaret called *fifteen* then *five* then *places*, and Winnie found a folding chair in a corner backstage with just enough light to read by. Scene by little scene unfolded without a miss. The actors played their parts and anticipated her. Whatever they felt offstage, they established a sympathetic rhythm under the lights. Whenever Winnie stepped into their holy space, she was the interloper, the one who inspired wariness. The unknown. The unsifted. She sensed the other actors' eyes and ears trained on her ready to pick up the pieces she might drop. But she omitted one line only. And it happened in the closet scene, when she was alone with Hank during the apparition of his father's ghost.

The ghost in the production was a voice over a loudspeaker. Hank turned to her, frantic. "Do you see nothing there?" he demanded. Winnie answered, "Nothing at all; yet all that is I see." Then Hank, "Nor did you nothing hear?" Winnie hesitated. She sat in amazement at his passion and beauty. He mistook her admiration for forgetfulness and like a speeding train he ran over her lovely line, "No, nothing but ourselves," and shouted, "Why, look you there how it steals away!"

She felt cheated.

And moments later when he turned his anger on her for sleeping with his uncle, he yanked the cameo from around her neck. True, it hung on a trick chain secured by a thread, but still she wept at the shock and violence of it and saw he was pleased to move her to tears.

In the final scene after she'd fallen from "the drink, the drink, oh, my dear Hamlet, the drink. I am poisoned," and after Michael scratched Hank with the poisoned poniard, he crawled over to her dead body and kissed her on the cleavage. "Wretched Queen, adieu," he said. In that moment, she knew what it felt like to rise from the dead, but she couldn't move because it was only a play. At the curtain call, Hank's bow was appropriately the last, and he took it, but then he turned upstage and reached for her and presented her like a gift to the audience. Lucy waited for Winnie in the lobby and cried when her sister appeared. Together, they waltzed out of the theater into the cold night and hailed a cab adjacent to the lighted dome of the Capitol. No matter she had to clean teeth in the morning. Nothing mattered that evening, the first evening she played Gertrude to Hank Brody's, *Hamlet*.

Winnie had known actors who devoted their lives to Shakespeare, in particular his tragedies, those lucky few who hung suspended in a state of acute perception and awe for at least the run of a show. The more bodies littering the stage as the last, usually rhyming, couplet, the more susceptible the actors were on stage and off. Every actor was aware of the perils of performing *Macbeth*, the darkest jewel in the Bard's box; they were notoriously beset by accidents both serious and ridiculous, in the theater and out. And so it was that Alice Langford missed the rest of the run, never to return again to that snake pit of a production.

And as far as Winnie's ability was concerned, the administration agreed that the understudy who cleaned teeth by day seemed up to the task at night and even had her moments. Anyway, that was the talk that trickled down to her.

She returned to the dental office and played the mouse. To avoid suspicion, she kept her evening appearances a secret until the following week when she announced her break and invited all her co-workers to the show. No one was mad at her. Even Carl insisted he come to see her play the Queen on the Hill.

Winnie wanted to freeze time, especially those moments she shared with Hank on stage. Jesus on the cross, she thought, I'm playing incest on top of committing a sin against the ninth commandment, the one about coveting thy neighbor's wife. Hank was married but rumors circulated about his serial carousing in the Capitol Hill bars most nights after the show came down. Why not carouse with her? And whenever she pondered that, she felt there was indeed something rotten in the state of Denmark. He was married, and she was sober. Her carousing days were long over. Still. There was always club soda. She wanted him off-stage whatever the circumstances and consequences. But he wasn't interested. He never asked.

With less than a week remaining, Misty's mother died and panic rippled through the company. Winnie, the reigning Queen of Elsinore, was still the official understudy for the role of Ophelia. How could she play two parts at once? There were too many overlapping scenes. Otherwise, management may have proposed double casting her. Everyone knew that a cursed production, probably Hank's doing, could rarely right itself. But a suitable remedy appeared in the form of a diminutive actress down from New York rehearsing the part of Hermia for the next show, *A Midsummer Night's Dream*. The little brunette model of ambition had just played Ophelia four months earlier in Cleveland and was happy and willing to go on.

Hank was deranged over the announcement of a second casting shuffle in three weeks. He gathered the cast on stage and delivered a venomous speech urging a cancellation of the matinee in question. He railed against the producer and pointed to Winnie as an example of their money saving tactics. "The fuckers," he shrieked. "They've got you working here on the cheap, and it's a crime. You ought to go to your union and complain. In the case of this bloody matinee, I advocate we take a vote and inform the pricks we won't go on."

But the company members who wished to remain company members thought the show must go on, and it did. Ophelia Number Two stepped into the part on the day of the funeral and had all her lines. How clever of her, Winnie thought, in a catty moment. Both Ophelias were petite and hailed from New York. Winnie was envious of both of them. When she was tired and thought hard about it, she hated them.

Misty returned for the Saturday evening performance and grieved for her father Polonius on stage as she'd done her real-life mother that morning. Her mad scene swelled to bursting. Fresh raw grief elevated her expression to genius. As Gertrude, Winnie watched it nightly, but that evening she wept until her nose ran like a stream. She turned discreetly upstage and wiped it on her velvet sleeve. Yes, Ophelia Number One soared in her madness over lost loved ones, and every actor on stage witnessed the gorgeous event. Some girls have all the luck, Winnie thought. And then she remembered at what cost to Misty and heartlessly, artistically reconsidered; some girls have all the luck.

The following day was Sunday, the final two performances. Winnie was despondent. Tomorrow he'd be gone on a flight back to England, and she would never see him again. Between the matinee and evening performances, she knocked on his dressing room door and presented him with a closing night gift. She'd found out from the actor who played Horatio that Hank liked brandy, so she'd splurged and bought him an expensive bottle. He lit up at the sight of it, thanked her warmly, and stashed it under his make-up table. She knew it wasn't her he was happy to see; it was the bottle. She bit her lip, wished him well, and left the room.

Why she hadn't waited until the end of the evening to give it to him haunted her silly for months after. And why did she, the one who'd quit drinking, buy booze for the drinker? It was a misdeed, like giving a pound of truffles to a diabetic. But she knew what he liked and she wanted him to be happy. Was it for her or him? She wanted him to fall in love with her at the sight of the brandy, but it was the drink that mattered, not the giver.

"He's loaded," Rosencrantz said to Guildenstern. They lingered in the wings; Winnie overheard them on her exit and cringed. My fault, she thought.

Hank made his entrance in the closet scene to confront Winnie with her sin. This was her favorite scene. It was long and physical. He was always passionate and stern with her. Part priest, part lover. He entered for the last time and seemed wilder than usual, with something amiss around his eyes. Or was it his hair? She hoped he was as desperate as she with the knowledge that this was it, their last opportunity for intimacy, tainted or not.

At the top of the scene upon hearing a voice behind the arras and believing it to be the King, Hank shouted as usual, "How now, a rat?" He unsheathed his heavy sword and stabbed the "rash intruding fool"—in reality a pillow behind the curtain— proclaiming, "Dead for a ducat, Dead." And then with untoward recklessness, he yanked the sword out of the pillow/body and lost his grip on the weapon's handle. Dumbfounded, he and Winnie watched it fly, not, by some lucky fluke, into the audience because it would have killed a patron or two. Instead, it flew across the entire length of the stage and disappeared through the stage left blacks into the wings where it hit the wall of the theater with a crash before it clattered to the floor.

"Oh, me what hast thou done?" Winnie gasped her line, not acting anymore.

He looked at her and responded, "Nay, I know not, is it the King?"

But she saw he was thinking hard about how and when he might run off and retrieve the weapon in the dark. He whipped the upstage curtain aside and conveniently discovered not a pillow but a fallen Polonius.

Hank sprung at her, commanding, "Leave wringing of your hands. Peace, sit you down and let me wring your heart, for so I shall if it be made of penetrable stuff . . ."

She was certain it was. Cupid laboring on his behalf had made it so.

He thrust her into the flimsy, Renaissance style chair and moved to exit after the sword. The force of the push and her weight on the chair sent it tipping backwards until it teetered on its two upstage legs. She hovered with her legs dangling off the floor in imminent danger of disaster. She cried out. He turned and watched. They both knew he was too far away to help her. She had to save herself.

She knew that Queens of Denmark didn't wear panty hose until modern times and the audience would cease to care about Shakespeare's drama if they saw her upended, legs and gown flung skyward, and her bottom exposed in control tops. Worse, if she fell over and broke her neck, they'd worry about her instead of Hamlet. With vanity, the play, and her life in peril, Winnie closed her eyes and threw all her weight forward. The chair crashed down on all four legs and when she opened her eyes, Hank was in place, sword in hand.

She was certain their combined adrenalin could have murdered a moose, yet they still had a long scene to play. Would she survive it? She rose on her next line and crossed to him, but the hem of her gown, trapped under the chair's front legs dragged it until the bottom of her skirt came apart. No, she thought, I won't live through this. And just as the scene seemed to careen into farce, Hank held her and played what remained of it with tenderness.

But it wasn't over. There was more fire to come. Hank had insulted Misty in undertones on stage during the play within the play. They were blocked to sit together on the floor with their backs to the audience. The entire company witnessed the scene and he mumbled obscenities throughout. At the second intermission, the young actor playing Fortinbras who was unabashedly in love with Misty, waited for Hank in his dressing room and threw the first punch. Hank hit back. Horatio ran down the hall at the first sound of the scuffle and separated them. As usual the on-stage relationships spilled off, and Horatio and Winnie were the only friends Hank had by the end of the run.

Winnie burned with guilt over the brandy until the final scene when Hank, mortally wounded, crawled to her and kissed her on the lips. If she hadn't been dead she'd have reached up and pulled him to her and held on so tight he would have missed his plane to London. The curtain fell, and she cried. How could she face not seeing him six nights and two afternoons a week? And what about the life and death stuff of the stage, the make believe *and* the real? God. All teeth and no Shakespeare was a prospect as bleak as mid-January.

The cab driver sailed through empty Sunday streets. She paid him and climbed the stairs to her apartment, her arms loaded with make-up bags, empty vases, cards, and souvenirs. When she'd slipped it into her purse, she told herself the costume department would never miss the beaded snood she'd worn as Queen of Elsinore. Winnie opened the door and saw the red light shining, even and steady on her Panasonic. No new messages.

She undressed, set her alarm clock for 6:30 AM, and crawled into the giant bed, her cat at her feet. She reviewed her glorious day and night. Tomorrow would dawn normal no matter the messages.

Originally from Ohio, Mary Kay Wulf currently resides in LA with her companion, a former freedom fighter from North Africa. After a long career in the performing arts, she earned an MFA at Antioch University LA, where she is a guest lecturer. Her stories and reviews have been published in *34th Parallel Magazine, Lunch Ticket, Drunk Monkeys*, and *Annotation Nation*.

Tamela Ritter

Quantifying Momentum

One. Two. Three. Four.

The telephone poles came in regular intervals now, one every 1.75 seconds. Mabel knew that meant her mom was driving. Her father's driving was more erratic and more determined by mood and destination. He stopped and slowed, gunned the engine and swerved but never did he go below 1.5 seconds between poles.

She looked at the map lying crumpled, folded and parched next to her. She had an almost uncontrollable need to open it up again and see how many inches they had gone since she'd last checked. Her fingers hovered over it, but as she looked to the passenger side where her father's head bobbed, fighting the lure of the monotonous road to pull him to sleep, she withdrew her hand back to her lap, back to her skinny thighs sticky with sweat. Instead she put the colored lines, stars and topographies of the map out of her mind and returned to counting telephone poles out the window.

One. Two. Three. Four.

Stealing peeks in the rearview mirror, Nadine hoped to catch her daughter's gaze, to share a reassuring smile. She knew her daughter was not like other girls. Not like other children. She had stopped caring, stopped listening to those so-called experts who told her what Mabel needed, what she should be doing. It was a phase, Nadine reasoned. Things that puberty and the forced transient life intensified. In the end, she knew her daughter would be fine.

So what if the girl had a few obsessions, if Mabel was obsessed with numbers—so was her father, who cared? She liked to avoid cracks—who didn't? She liked to study maps and road signs and often wondered aloud if the billboards toting the World's Largest this or that were all they said to be, and how none of them had been so far.

Besides, it wasn't really the girl's fault that she needed maps. If anyone spent as much time staring out windows at scenery that was always moving, always changing, they'd look for something that was solid too. Of course she looked for something that stayed where it was; markers that weren't pulled away every time she was sure she had finally arrived. Things like the dots that labeled the towns that she would never live in.

Her daughter finally pulled her eyes from the road and they shared a look through the mirror. Nadine sighed and pushed the thoughts of their current reality out of her mind and instead focused on what their life would be when they finally found a place to settle, a place that lived up to the promise. They would have a yard, she dreamed, a kitchen with full-sized appliances, bedrooms with no bad art on the walls. They would start again and all the headaches, all the frustration from the past year would be forgotten. *Soon*, she thought, pushing her damp hair from her eyes and rolling down the window. She knew the chills would set in soon but she pushed those from her mind too. She was stifled and was having trouble breathing. All she needed was some fresh air, she tried to convince herself.

One. Two. Three. Four.

Brewster turned his head to the newly opened window. The lines of the upholstery itched a white puckered zigzag against his flushed, sweaty cheek. It was roasting in the car; the air conditioner was a joke. Everything about this car was a joke. He cursed under his breath, opening his eyes and squinting against the sun's glare off the pavement.

He hated the car, but it was the only thing they had to take them from one failed job to the whisper of another. He hadn't wanted his life to be this. These open roads and broken promises. It didn't matter that the rest of the country was also in this shift that seemed to start with a slight tilt and was now, for him, a full-fledged slide down the wrong side of his life.

These days, his highest achievement was that he never took his frustrated anxiety out on his wife or child. He wasn't going to make it any harder than it already was, living from town to falling-apart town. One day— one day soon, everything would turn around. The world would see his value. Until then he kept his family moving, always forward and in the back of his mind he made lists.

1. Find a job
2. Find a home
3. Find Mabel a school
4. Get health insurance

Those were the top items on the list that just kept getting longer and longer. When he was in an ironic mood he thought about how lucky he was that he was an accountant and liked large numbers. He wasn't the only one, he thought, as he heard Mabel's mumbled counting in the back seat. He sat up and rubbed at his eyes, trying not to drift back to sleep. He tried not to join his daughter in the counting as the long white lines swiped past him.

"Where are we?" he asked.

"Twelve miles out of Pecos," Mabel answered.

"Twelve miles?" Brewster asked, looking back at her and then to his wife.

Nadine saw his confused look and said, "I go the speed limit," as if that answered everything. He still looked slightly dazed so she elaborated. "Time times speed equals—"

"Distance," Brewster interrupted, finally understanding and sighing. "That's my little mathematician."

Mabel didn't respond; she was too busy looking out the window and counting.

Brewster studied his wife instead. The bags under her eyes were a constant these days and she had started taking on a bony look.

"You feeling okay?" he asked.

"Fine, just a headache. I think it's my eyes. It's too bright. The glare. The road."

He studied her some more, subconsciously adding better nutrition to his list under the health and welfare bullet point.

"How long until we're out of this godforsaken state?" he asked, turning back to his daughter.

Never taking her eyes off the road, she pointed out the window. Brewster followed her direction just in time to see the large sign reading, "Welcome to New Mexico: The Land of Enchantment."

"Great. You want to let me drive, or are you ready to find a vacancy?" he asked his wife, feeling instantly better as they crossed the border. Texas had been a bust. A bust that went on for miles and miles and miles. Now he could cross that off his to do list. He had gotten out.

One. Two. Three. Four.

Their room had orange furniture and paisley curtains that smelled like they'd been hanging long before the ban on smoking had been enforced. After five minutes, Mabel's jitters kicked in and she felt the overwhelming need to get out. She made the excuse of wanting to get ice. Her mother lined the chipped brown plastic bucket with the flimsy plastic bag that was sticky against the bottom and told Mabel to come right back.

Nodding her head, she skipped out the room. She looked out to the highway, watching the few cars zoom by, and followed them with her gaze until their shimmer and haze danced on the horizon. She scanned the lot and the building, trying to remember where the man with the toothpick in his mouth and the lazy eye who gave them the key told them everything was located. There was always a guy with a toothpick and a lazy eye. They were as consistent as the stars on the map indicating capitals.

She saw the door next to the office and remembered peeking in while her father filled out the paperwork. There was an ice machine in there along with a soda machine, a washer and dryer, a few video games and a scratched up pool table.

Looking down at her shoes, like she always did when she walked, she counted the times her feet touched the ground between each square of the cement and avoided the cracks. If she saw that she would be landing on an odd number in that last step, she would take a smaller one, or a larger one to bring it to evens. She never felt right if she took odd steps, like the world had shifted on its axis for a moment and she was unsteady. The stairs were different; she had no control over those, so she thundered down them, giving them no more thought then she did to her nighttime dreams. The sidewalks on the lower level and the tarred driveway shortcut were a jumble of cracks and divots. She looked around to make sure no one would notice before she began to carefully tiptoe her way to the ice machine, still counting every step.

One. Two. Three. Four.

"What is she doing?" Brewster asked, pulling apart the curtains to watch his daughter's odd movements. Nadine walked to the window and looked out too.

"She's always done that."

"She has?"

"Yeah. I can't remember a time where she didn't avoid cracks and count steps."

"Really? Why?"

Nadine shrugged. "I'm sure as soon as she figures it out, she'll let us know."

If he wasn't so preoccupied worrying about the mystery and neurosis that was his daughter, he would have started questioning when his wife had become so flippant about their daughter's oddities. One problem at a time was his motto. Today, right now, it was his daughter. The one he could do something about. Perhaps.

He returned to his To Do List. Sometimes it got even more overwhelming than the panic of their current living situation. He never would have thought that would happen. The realization of being jobless, homeless and listless had filled him with dread and a soul-sucking fear in the beginning. But now, all he had was time and anxiety.

Right now, the top on the list was his daughter. She needed a home; a school that she could attend for more than a few months at a stretch, the length of time from him finding a job and the time it was announced it would either disappear, become temporary all of a sudden, or wouldn't even cover the expense it had taken to get there.

Stability was definitely something she needed. He saw that in the way she became obsessed with things like counting telephone poles and trees, the way she studied clouds for hours in the back of their car, the way she studied maps like they were a magical parchment that told her secrets on their faded and folded pages. She also needed something to occupy her time, something to do besides worry about where she would sleep at night, where they would finally land, where she would finally be normal.

They were all on the list. Were their own subset actually, under the title: Fix Mabel.

One. Two. Three. Four.

Nadine watched her husband look at the dusty window at the puzzle of their daughter as if she were a brand new spectacle he'd never witnessed before. She sighed and wondered when he had stopped paying attention. She didn't really blame him, of course she didn't. He had a lot to think about and she knew that he took the responsibility of them all on his chest. He'd grown up with the Man of the House Brings Home the Bacon mentality and she knew it was hard for him.

She came over and kissed him on the top of his head. She wasn't even sure if he noticed. He didn't say anything, and his gaze stayed fixed on where their daughter had finally disappeared inside the office. For a moment, like a lot of moments when she saw her daughter walk out of her sight, Nadine wanted to run after her, be with her, make sure she would survive. The moment passed though.

"She'll be okay." She wasn't sure if she wanted to ease his mind or her own. "I'm going to go and wash the road off me. You'll wait to eat until I'm done?"

"Hmmm?" he asked, looking away from the window.

"I said I'm going to take a quick shower. Wait for me to have the sandwiches?"

"Sure. Of course."

She smiled sadly at him and went to her luggage, rifling through some things looking for her toiletries. She wondered when they had gotten so polite with each other. She guessed it was right after they'd had their major blow up, drag 'em out fight. The one that they both surely thought would have ended them. Instead, it got them both to shrug helplessly, pack all the small U-Haul trailer would hold and move from town to town.

Starting the tub's water to get it to the right temperature for her shower, she took off her clothes and looked at her reflection. Rust flaked around the edges of the mirror and Nadine thought that was about right. Fitting almost. She leaned in, making sure that her jutting hip bones didn't touch the sink. The whole bathroom felt *unclean* and she would have laughed at the irony of it but she was too tired. She had gotten used to feeling slightly unclean the moment she stepped out of the shower—and once in San Antonio when the water had felt thick—during a shower.

It was only a matter of time before they would have a place of their own again. She knew it. Could feel it. Sometimes the excitement of their possible futures almost made her shout out. She only stopped herself because she would frighten Mabel and confuse Brewster. She kept it to herself. Close to her heart. Things couldn't get worse. That was the mantra she clung too.

They had sold the house right after Brewster had been laid off from his high-paying corporate gig that they had all hated for the way it took him away from the family. Now there was no getting away from each other even if they had wanted to, and sometimes they did, desperately. Thankfully, the sell went through right before the housing market fell apart. Another set of ironies she hadn't the strength to laugh about. The loss of their house had been the last bit of good luck they would have for a long time.

She switched the water to spray and sighed at the sad little stream of water that spritzed out of the head. Why were showers of all the cheap motels in the country exactly the same?

One. Two. Three. Four.

Mabel filled the bucket with ice and was about to walk out the door when she stopped to look at the pool table. All the balls sat on the green felt in a perfect triangle. All the little circles with numbers in the center were facing up and all the stripes were facing the same way in the pattern of solid, strip, solid, stripe. She was mesmerized with the exactitude and perfection of the table.

She reached into her pocket and caressed her newest talisman-- a pack of matches from Senor Taco, the Abilene family style restaurant they had eaten at two days ago. She liked to collect matches and each day she would pull one match out of each row in order to make the rows even every three days. She would light the match, hold it between her fingers and count how long she could hold it before she had to drop it or blow it out. She wasn't very good at it yet. She could never wait long enough to feel anything; the fear of what the fire would sting like always overtook her too soon. This one still had 16 matches in it. Thinking of that distracted her from the pool table. But then her father came in and she pulled her hand out of her pocket quickly.

"Hey sport. Wanna play a game?" he asked, reaching for a pool stick.

"No," she answered too loudly, too strangely.

"Okay," he answered, tossing the stick onto the table, upsetting the balls violently, sending one of them into a corner pocket.

"I didn't mean it," she said, then looked at the disrupted perfection forlornly. "I would really like to play a game."

When the balls were all in their holes and the game was over, she would be able to bring them out and make everything right again, she thought as she watched him organize the chaos once again.

One. Two. Three. Four.

Nadine got under the water and sighed again. For what it lacked in strength it made up for in temperature. It was heavenly warm and she knew it sounded weird, but it *smelled* good. It didn't have that bleach and chlorine scent some places had and the rusty, stale smell of some of the others. Instead it smelled fresh and clean. Her spirits soared as she stood under the water long enough for her hair to get wet. Then she grabbed the little sampler shampoo she still had from the last place they stayed that had provided the finer things like shampoo, soap and even shower caps. She tried not to remember what the feel of a full size bottle full of cleanser felt like in her wet hands, the thrill of its slippery texture sliding along her palm almost falling to the ground with a splash. There were many things she tried to forget. Many things she pushed to the back of her mind. Like how she was tired; all the time exhausted, sore and feverish.

One. Two. Three. Four.

They chalked the sticks laboriously and he showed her to stand with legs spread out, bend at the waist, stick between middle and pointer finger, grasped loosely at the end to easily slide it, the thumb keeping it steady. He showed her about angles, inertia, momentum, cause and effect. He showed her about stripes and solids, scratches and jumps and how important the white ball was and what the rules were for where it could go when. She listened and watched him, not even blinking for fear of missing something vital. She was most fascinated with the angles and the friction. The numbers on the balls themselves intrigued her too. But besides the black 8 ball, he didn't mention that the numbers were important. So, like so many other things, the numbers and patterns were important only to her.

One. Two. Three. Four.

"What are you doing?" he asked.

She looked up to him, this daughter of his that mystified and intrigued him. "Hitting the six into the side pocket, why? Do I have to say at every turn or only for the eight?"

"Well, I guess it depends who you're playing. I just call the eight, but some of the more by-the-rules people want you to call out all your balls and they only count the ones that actually go where you planned for them to go."

"Oh. How would they go into pockets you weren't planning for?" she asked, confused. She always did that; always focused on the wrong part of any conversation.

"It happens all the time," he answered. "Not everyone can factor just right the angles of things. Some people get lucky."

She gave him that look again. As if he was talking about things that didn't make sense. He supposed *luck* was something she wasn't familiar with.

"But I was just asking what you were doing because, well, wouldn't it be an easier shot if you went for the twelve ball instead of the six?"

He pointed to indicate what he meant. She studied both, shrugged and angled herself, and, rimming the white ball against the side at a sharp corner, hit the six ball and sent it exactly where she wanted it to go. He wondered if the challenge of it was why she did it. He smiled at his fast learner and thought to himself, if nothing else worked, he could take Mabel to the pool halls and make some scratch that way.

One. Two. Three. Four.

Her shower was short and haphazard.

She never spent too much time thinking about her body. Not since finding a bizarre bump on the top of her head a few months ago. This troubled her even more now that they were uninsured and living off what they had made from selling the house and their second car. The money would only last so long and those guaranteed jobs that Brewster could find every year around tax time were a long way away.

It was better not to know. Worrying about things that couldn't be fixed, couldn't even be mended was futile. She had more things to think about then odd bumps, shortness of breath and an exhaustion that she couldn't shake. She attributed it to the cheap motels, bad food and the hours sitting in a car with hardly any shocks and bad air-conditioning.

She got out of the bath and called out to the other room. "Are you still waiting? I'm just getting dressed. One more minute."

There was no answer. She wrapped a towel around her torso which barely fell past the curve of her butt and barely got around her skinny frame.

The room was empty.

She was horrified to discover the curtains wide open and the idea of the whole parking lot seeing her in a towel made her tiptoe to the window. Before she closed it all the way she checked to make sure the car was still there; of course it was. They wouldn't leave without telling her. *Why would you even think that*, she admonished herself as she shut the blinds and went back to the bathroom to get dressed.

As she went, she glanced at the large bed. It really did look comfortable. There was the usual flowery patterned thin cover, but there was also a thick solid yellow blanket folded across the foot of the bed and the pillows actually looked as if they weren't a hundred years old and deflated. Suddenly she felt like putting on a nightshirt and sliding under the covers for a moment or two of rest. Just a moment. She was just so tired.

All the time, tired.

One. Two. Three. Four.

"So, what do you like to do?" her father asked.

"What do you mean?"

"For fun? What did you used to do with your friends? What did you do with your free time?"

Mabel thought about this, what did she do? Those days when she was free of constant parental attention seemed so long ago. Obviously she had filled them, but for the life of her she couldn't remember how. That was a dangerous answer though, she knew that. She knew he found her odd.

She shrugged. "We just played."

"Really? What did you play?"

She thought back to the few times that she did have friends. "Dolls and house. Sometimes we went to the wade pool, but we got too big for that. So we'd go the river. Just to get wet."

"That sounds like fun."

"It was," she answered. If it happened like she remembered. She couldn't trust her memory though.

"We should go swimming."

"Really?" she asked.

Suddenly, just the thought of swimming, of being out past her depth, going under and being in another world where she couldn't see or hear anything but her own blood rushing in her veins excited her.

"Definitely. We don't have to be in Denver until Tuesday. We should absolutely go swimming. Let's eat first and see if your mom wants to go. See if the clerk knows a good place."

She looked at him getting excited too and smiled. She couldn't remember the last time they'd both been happy at the same time.

One. Two. Three. Four.

If his daughter skipped around awkwardly to avoid cracks, or took odd sized steps along the sidewalk as they walked back to the room, he didn't notice. He felt better as a father then he had in a long time. He almost hoped his wife wouldn't want to join them. Not because he didn't enjoy her company, or doing things as a family. It was just that when Nadine was around, his daughter fluttered around her, waiting for her to set a pace, a mood before Mabel would act. He wanted to see what his daughter was like on her own.

They came to the room and thankfully they were quiet because Nadine was under the covers fast asleep. She was curled tightly in a ball as if terrified to be awoken or maybe frozen and conserving space to gather heat.

"Shhhh," he whispered, going over to the bed slowly and quietly to make sure she was really asleep. He had an idea. "Feel like a picnic?"

Mabel's eyes lit up and she nodded.

"Write a note for mom while I pack us up," he said.

He put the sandwiches back in the bag they had come in. Took the bag of ice and put it into the plastic bag that held the sodas. It was right before they were to leave that he realized he had packed up Nadine's food as well. He took one of the bologna and cheese sandwiches and a diet coke back out and sat them next to the note. The condensation from the soda slid down the can, but they were already tiptoeing out the door.

One. Two. Three. Four.

Nadine woke with a cry. She rolled onto her other side and whimpered. There was an excruciating pain ripping through her body, starting at her abdomen and spreading in all directions. She took strong, deep breathes, even though they tore through her chest. She thought she heard gravel outside of a car pulling out. She looked around in a panic and froze. The ice bucket was back in the room.

Where had they gone? She cried out their names, sounding even more pathetic than she felt, hoping they would hear her desperation. No answer.

She tried to unfurl and lay out straight, but the pain came in waves, heaving and receding. It didn't matter if she was in a ball or lying flat, though she felt safer in the ball. She guessed it had something to do subconsciously with the womb and the safety it provided. *My subconscious obviously never met my mother.*

Slowly, she slid to the end of the bed, taking deep breathes to manage the pain. Hiding and swallowing pain was something she'd become an expert at. After a moment, with her feet dangling over the side of the bed, she rolled over and just before she was about to fall, she pulled up and found herself, almost shockingly, on her feet. She reached out for the table so she didn't fall face first into it.

There was a note there, but it had been soaked by the soda's sweating. She moved the almost lukewarm bottle over and picked up the paper, hoping to be able to decipher something from its smudge. All she could make out was that it had been written by her daughter. She scanned the empty parking lot. She was alone. Deserted in this shithole motel and she was going to die.

She sat down at one of the slick, fake leather seats around the small table. The sight of the wrapped sandwich made her stomach roll in its juices.

Part of it was hunger, but as she peeled back the wrapper the smell made her gag and grab her mouth to stop herself from throwing up. She swallowed the bile along with her growing panic. They couldn't have, wouldn't have gone too far. Would they?

No, they'd be back.

One. Two. Three. Four.

He hadn't enjoyed himself like this in so long. It was almost like he was his old self again; as if he didn't have a care in the world beyond the moment and the welfare of his daughter. He watched her delicately negotiate the gravely, rough unseen and even that made him smile, wondering if she was counting each rock, each leaf that floated along the river's surface. Today, right now, he hoped so. Today, right now, he saw her peculiarities as unique quirks and that was much more splendid. He trudged in front of her and turned to take her hands and guide her safely to the depth of the middle of the river. The water was cool and refreshing and seemed to awaken them both.

They swam for a bit, but they splashed around and lay in the hot sun for longer. He could have stayed like this forever. But Nadine would worry. So, after a few hours, when they were both completely dried off and completely wiped out, they hiked back to the dirt road where the car was waiting.

"Good day," Mabel whispered just loud enough for him to hear.

He smiled. "Yes, good day."

One. Two. Three. Four.

The view was different from the front seat. She didn't get to sit there very often; the three of them were usually together. But there in the front, the window spread out in front of her and the road seemed stretched out, never ending. The dread of the unknown was soon outweighed by the possibility of the mountains, the sky and the gloriously puffed clouds. Oh, if all days could be like this one. If every day she sat in this position and welcomed the world, new and exciting. Instead of the back seat where she craned her neck to see the same thing, the same trees, the same mailboxes and the same telephone poles.

For the first couple of miles, she even forgot to count. There was too much to see. But then the sky turned gray and ominous. A moment later with a flash of lightning and the rain began falling. When the windshield wipers began flapping back and forth and back and forth, the almost hypnotic pull of her cocoon of numbers called to her as her eyes drooped.

"One . . . two . . . three . . . four."

Nadine's shrieks had become sobs and then settled once again into whimpers before she tried to move from the bed to get help. She couldn't remember how she had gotten back into the bed, had curled herself back into the fetal position. But now she crawled back out and went for her phone. She didn't know why she hadn't thought of it earlier. She blamed the horrific pain.

Panting and sweaty by the time she made it to her purse; she dialed her husband's cell phone number and started to cry. It went straight to voice mail. A new wave of pain rolled over her and she lay on the floor writhing. When it receded enough for her to think, she did the only thing she could, insurance be damned. 9-1-1.

"One . . . two . . . three . . . four . . . "

Her voice was barely audible and Brewster found himself counting with her as he scanned the storm-darkened sky and wet road in front of him, trying to time her numbers with some event. At first he thought it was the swipe of the windshield wiper but it didn't sync anymore. Her monotone was slower than the flap of the wiper. He peeked at her and saw that she was actually asleep. She was counting in her sleep. He imagined what type of sheep visited his daughter, probably ones with little circles of numbers in a row of stripes and solids.

He smiled and tried not to continue counting, he knew that was a bad idea while driving. Bad things could happen. But, to be that peaceful and innocent—so free of responsibility, to . . . just . . . be . . . able . . . to . . . close . . . his . . . eyes . . . and . . .

One... Two... Three . . .

Tamela J. Ritter likens herself a wandering storyteller. Her stories and heart will forever reside in the West, while her feet have been rooted in the East. Her soul though, will always travel along the dusty, winding American highways, looking for shenanigans and whatnot. Her first book *From These Ashes* was published with Battered Suitcase Press in 2013. She hopes to have a short story collection published later this year.

Visit her online at: www.tamelajritter.com
Or via social media: @tamela_j www.facebook.com/TamelaJRitter

Sara Brooks

Driving to Boca Raton

200 mg of Lamictal, little blue pill.
Used in the treatment of seizures and bipolar disorder.
Possible side effects: Depression, irritability, fever, bruising, or muscle
weakness.
Actual side effects: God-like delusions of being cured, compulsively saying
the phrase "suicidal ideation" because it sounds fun, fear of silence, paranoia.
Take 1 daily at bedtime.

I sometimes worry I'm only as interesting as my last manic high.
When I'm manic, the wind feels sharper on my skin.
I can taste it on my tongue, sweet and dangerous
like maple trees on fire.

When I'm manic, I drive around at night,
with the windows down, even in the dead of winter.
I venture far into the middle of nowhere,
frantic and desperate,
like a wolf on the edge of starvation.
When I return home to my house on the mountain,
it twinkles in the dark,
like a ship lit by flickering candles,
riding on dark waves a hundred miles offshore.

Every three months, I receive the Eucharist from a tall blonde man in a white
coat.
My drug-store, blue-blooded, Coors Light, American Jesus;
his palms leaving smears of blood on my little orange bottles.

He preaches every day to his congregation:
little old ladies with aching joints,
kids with sore throats,
and bipolar brunettes with thick glasses and inferiority complexes.

His benediction is always the same
"Take with food, take without food.
Don't drink; don't smoke.
Do you have any questions?

Do you have any questions?
Do you have any —"

Questions? Yeah, I have a few.
Why do I still wake up every day wanting rip my skin apart at the seams,
to expose all the tissue and bone and machinery —
I want proof it is still functioning.

Why do I wake up shaking,
and sit on the edge of my bed, head in my hands,
mentally listing the pros and cons of jumping off an overpass?

It'd have to be high up. You can't half-ass your own suicide.

Since I was 10, I've lost myself for seconds, minutes, hours,
dreaming of superheroes and vampires and werewolves and witches
and any number of supernatural creatures.
I think it is their power I envy so much.
Their ability to change their circumstances through absolute force.
This is what makes the world go round.
"You have an active imagination,"
my first therapist told me.
No, if I had active imagination,
I could imagine myself happy in this world.
I could imagine myself with domain and control over my life.

But this idea is more foreign to me than beasts howling at the moon,
baying and crying out for blood.

My car is idling in the pharmacy pickup lane.
"Nope, no questions."
I smile and take the bag from him,
ignoring the red spots that have soaked into the packaging
from the thorns digging into his head.

900 mg of Lithium
Three white pills.
Used for the prevention of manic episodes of bipolar disorder.
Possible side effects: nausea, dizziness, muscle weakness, fatigue, intense
thirst, and a fine tremor.
Actual side effects: Make loud love professions at 3 a.m., becoming deeply
possessive of things I cannot possess, intense self-loathing.
Take daily at bedtime.

The best first date I have ever been on
involved a car accident.

Matt was blonde, a blue-eyed Navy boy.
Tall with tattoos and a big, goofy grin;
I was in love the minute I first saw him.
We walked down the docks in Norfolk,
looking at the decommissioned war ships.
Hulking goliaths slowly becoming more and more useless,
testaments to how size used to equal might.
It doesn't anymore.
We kill with glorified remote-controlled planes,
weaponized children's toys
terrorizing people in foreign lands
and making them fear the sky.

We used to think we could rule the seas
if we just put something big enough in them.
We forgot that in the timeline of life on Earth,
the ocean has us beat by a few million years.
It was here before us and it will be here after,
but it still beckons us forth to worship at its shores,
only to teach us time and time again that our offerings mean nothing
to a merciless god,
a ruthless Titan of eternity and sand.

We heard the unmistakable sound of metal on metal
but when I looked up, my failed tamer of the seas was already gone,
running up the street to help a boozy young girl
who had just wrapped her Trailblazer around a tree.

I loved him; I still do.
But I hated myself; I still do.
He knew both those things
so he declined to question why I squirreled him away in his barracks,
clinging to him at night like a dragon hoarding gold.

Terrified to lose one of the few pretty things I had
that made me feel alive.

It was sweet and timid and mutually gratifying
but progressively turned sharper

as he pinned me down by my wrists.
I felt crucified under his gaze,
regretful and angry and terrified
as we both realized where the eventual end would leave us:
Scared and alone with no way back to each other.

He got stationed on some island in the middle of nowhere
doing something for the national security of who gives a shit.

If anyone ever tells you being in love is all happiness
and comfort –
run.
They're lying.

Being in love is akin to drowning,
but you're supposed to help each other
learn to breathe underwater.
I never could get the hang of it,
so I clung to Matt like a barnacle attached to a ship,
but as he sailed away
I clung harder until eventually I lost my grip
and sank.

300 mg Wellbutrin XL.
1 white pill
Used for the treatment of depression.
Possible side effects: Seeing halos around lights, seeing or hearing things that
are not there, feeling like people are against you, sudden increase in energy,
racing thoughts, trouble sleeping, thoughts of hurting yourself, worsening
depression, severe agitation or confusion.
Actual side effects: See above.
Take 1 daily in the morning.

My cousin overdosed four weeks ago.
I remember washing dishes last Christmas
while everyone else stayed at the table,
and I told him that an addict is an addict is an addict –
no matter what you shove in your mouth or in your veins.
Some people just pick less brutal methods so
they can hide them under their starched collars and manicured fingernails.
They're just as repulsive as us, just as dirty;
the only difference is they refuse to see it.

He was 22, clean for almost two years.
I haven't talked about him in depth yet.
I think I'm still in that weird limbo state of shock
where I'm stunned and offended that
life would throw me another curveball
when it already knows I still can't manage even to hold the bat right.

30 hours seems so short.
Barely more than a day, really.
But when you drive from Virginia to Boca Raton, Florida,
it's an eternity.
If you've never been to Boca Raton,
let me paint you a picture.

Inside the marshy, swampy shithole that is the state of Florida
is another, deeper shithole.
A city that has industrialized death.
The only thing its two subsets of residents,
drug addicts and old people,
can seem to agree on.
We drove through the night to clean out his room
and let me tell you,
until you have to walk into a halfway house with a black trash bag
to get the clothes of a kid you spent 22 years of your life with;
until you have to pile his possessions up,
strung out from 14 hours in a beat up suburban;
until you have to tip-toe around the spot on the carpet where they found him,
needle in his arm after 2 years sober;
until then
you don't get to tell me he's in a better place.
He's with God; he's no longer suffering.
Save your platitudes and bullshit –
they do nothing for the people stuck here in the aftermath.
They do nothing for the people who have to walk through the floodwaters,
the razed towns,
the rubble, the destruction.

You will never recover.
You cannot grow back that missing piece of you
that will for ever be prisoner in a flophouse in fucking Boca Raton.

If God was merciful, he would help rebuild that part of you,
but God is not merciful;

he is vengeful and he loves killing.
If he didn't, he wouldn't do so much of it.
But he does it day after day after day after day,
in ways more spectacular and glorious than the last.
Maybe it's punishment.

We don't worship like we used to,
with violence and sacrifices and earth soaked with blood.
We answer only to ourselves now,
and this has made God wrathful and jealous and angry.
So he has made us subservient to something else:
Booze, drugs, sex, food, money.

If you haven't found yours yet,
you will.

And if you don't, don't worry.
It'll find you.

Sara Brooks is a 27-year-old (don't remind her) aspiring editor and coffee
aficionado living in the greater Northern Virginia area. She's currently
employed with the Department of Homeland Security and works out of our
nation's capital. Sara graduated from Christopher Newport University with a
B.A., double majoring in both English Writing and English Literature. Her
academic focuses included creative nonfiction, American slave politics,
feminist literature, and modernist writers (she's got a thing for Ernest
Hemingway). In 2014, Sara was invited to present her academic research on
the literary merit of Harlem Renaissance writer Claude McKay at the Paideia
Conference, representing the CNU English Department. Sara finished her
academic career with her senior thesis on the theology and psychosexuality of
Hemingway (seriously, she's got a problem). In addition to garnering several
literary magazine publications, Sara won 2nd place in the Virginia State Poetry
contest for her poem *Red*. Sara is currently watching every Marvel TV show
she can get her greedy mitts on and is always in some state of re-reading the
Harry Potter series. She likes superheroes (Captain America), antiheros (The
Punisher), amaretto sours, unreasonably loud music, gangly, dark-haired
dudes, and her dog, Lia.

Scott Davis Howard

One Knight and Two Faces: An Ominous Arthurian Adventure
As told by Aelfric the Entertainer

*Settle into your cushions (or benches, if you're able)—rest your elbows upon the table. Curl your fists 'round tankards and horns, and ready yourselves for a fine feast of lore. . .
Tonight—in this very hall—you've the privilege and pleasure to be entertained by Aelfric, bard beyond measure! In front of flickering firelight, with ale on your lips, I will your good cheer and merriment eclipse. A legend, it is, that I have to share, of Mordred and Gawain, who'd better beware! 'Tis a nightmare tale full of terror and rage, monsters and betrayal, the worst of the age, and I tell it better than most anyone else—better than Mordred, than even Malory himself. And I'll tell it with style—with themes and allusions, symbols, and footnotes to limit confusion. I'll begin on a summer day in north Wales, the isle of Anglesey, four men in bright mail, shore to their rear, pine-woods ahead, upon a high hill—needles green, trunks red. Sand blows in their eyes, carried by the sea breeze, up through the moaning, creaking red trees. Now, lend me an ear, listen up, if you please. . .*

Mordred shifted uncomfortably in his saddle. The twisting, turning ascent of this ridge, in the intense heat of the descending midsummer sun, was difficult. Ahead of him, Gringolet, Gawain's young, white charger, let out a determined snort as it weaved around a tall red-barked trunk, spindled with broken limbs. The trunk's long bar of shadow passed along the horse's flank, orange needle-litter shifted under its broad hooves, and a pinecone trundled down the incline. Following in single file, Mordred turned the same corner, switching back to lessen the angle of the climb. The boredom of this journey was nearly as painful to him as the chaffing on his thighs. As always, Gawain rode ahead, his face implacable. Behind, two men at arms, purple-clad in the Orkney house colors, led a packhorse burdened with a cumbersome load of kindling and firewood.

"Brother," Mordred began, turning to Gawain, "I've been studying your uncle, *my* father[1]. Everyone says that he's a good man and a strong king, but I'm not sure."

Gawain slowed. "About which? His goodness or his strength?"

"His strength, obviously," Mordred replied. "But to my way of thinking, the two are linked."

"Correct," Gawain smiled, his tone becoming insufferably instructional. "King Arthur's goodness—his virtue—makes him strong. It binds his followers to him and brings upon him and his kingdom the blessings of God. As my squire and as Arthur's son, you can only hope to emulate his attributes as you mature."

"Perhaps," Mordred responded, "but the more I observe him—and others, too—the more it seems to me that strength and weakness are fatally connected. For example, father's virtue, his best attribute, is also his greatest weakness. It blinds him to others' flaws, their plots, their lies. It makes him

---

[1] For those of you new to Arthurian romance, a few details might help: Mordred and Gawain are both central figures. First, Gawain is the son of King Lot of Orkney and Lady Morgause. Morgause is the half-sister of King Arthur, sharing the same mother, but different fathers (the story is long and complex—I'll spare you). Gawain has three brothers, Agravain, Gaheris, and Gareth, all of whom are Knights of the Round Table. Gawain is eldest and most prominent, having at least some role in every major Arthurian tale. He is King Arthur's nephew, and one of the king's most trusted knights. Mordred is also a son of Morgause. Mordred's father, however, is King Arthur, so he and Gawain are half-brothers. His story is… well… unfortunate. Here's the gist: due to the magical machinations of a witch named Morgan le Fay (who is, in fact, Morgause's sister), Arthur was deceived into impregnating his half-sister (yes, I know). This means Mordred is also Gawain's first cousin. The family relationships get more complex from there (not quite on Oedipus' level, but you take my meaning). I could go into more detail, but this should suffice for the present.

susceptible. It begs to be abused."

Gawain shook his head. "If virtue were a flaw, my youthful squire, then God would be at the mercy of the devil. Yet," he gestured around himself, "it is plainly not so. The benevolent sun still shines on all."

Mordred sighed. "The religious defense is always impenetrable," then mumbled under his breath: "an impervious armor of studied ignorance." He raised his voice again to conversational levels, "I still think he's susceptible. I've seen skeptics and they don't believe anyone without proof. Seems to me that's safer than blind faith—the foolish belief in the virtue of strangers—at least in this life it is, if not the afterlife."

"Liars," Gawain observed grimly, "never believe anyone else, and so no one believes in them."

"Trust me," Mordred continued, "my father will be trapped by virtue one day, by faith in the wrong person, belief in a lie, or through trust misplaced. I see it coming, clear as the sun will set." He gestured behind them, where the gray ocean could still (barely) be discerned through the trees.

"Strength is weakness," Gawain scoffed, "is a typical teenage paradox. I very much enjoyed that kind of thing as a youth, and thought myself learned when I invented one."

"Don't believe me." Mordred retorted, annoyed at Gawain's gentle mocking. "As you will, but you're susceptible, too. Your greatest assets, loyalty and courtesy, may be your undoing."

"I would leave this world smiling if I should be so lucky as to die in defense of them. They are worth the sacrifice."

"Observe," Mordred said, emphatic. "Father sent you here to negotiate with Lord Gruffudd to bring Gwynedd under his banner. You *loyally* obey. Your orders instruct you to do *whatever* it takes. You get here and, Lo! Gruffudd's only daughter has been captured. 'A great opportunity to prove the value of Arthur's knights,' you think, so you offer assistance, both because of your loyalty and your vow of courtesy to save women from all danger. The *choice* was inescapable. Was it ever a choice at all?"

"No, certainly not. We must do what's right." Gawain stopped his horse and turned to face Mordred. "We have a responsibility to set an example for others. That is the essence of what it means to be a knight of the Round Table. We embody our king's ideals."

Mordred made a face. "Don't you see? This could all be a ploy, a plot to destroy you... and *me*, for that matter. The son of a king is a prime target. And yet, you glibly ride into it, self-assured in your righteous nobility— that and the power of your sword-arm. It makes you ridiculously predictable, brother."

"It makes me right," Gawain responded, "which is the only way I want to be." He clucked to his horse, resuming their movement.

Mordred sighed, frustrated. "Are you sure we're still on the creature's trail?" He changed the subject. "Do you suppose that this *Margaret* is even alive?"

"I am certain of both," Gawain turned his pale blue eyes to scan ahead. His blonde shoulder-length hair brushed against the purple cloth of the felted cape on his shoulder. "Edgar is an excellent yeoman, a proper forester. He says the trail is as plain as day, and we haven't yet seen blood, bones, nor any evidence of feeding." He pulled his horse ahead, weaving between two outcrops of jagged slate.

As they crested the hill, Mordred spurred his roan gelding, drawing even with (though at a lower height than) his elder stepbrother for a second time. "But I've never heard of a gwyll venturing this far, nor of one keeping a prisoner. Certainly, they do take food with them—by that, of course, I mean kill a man and flee with all or some of the corpse, but this one has stolen a lord's daughter and is leading us on a chase. It's odd. Makes me uneasy."

"Indeed," Gawain replied, "yet even if she weren't alive, we would have no choice but to continue—we cannot return to Aberfraw empty handed and tell Lord Gruffudd that Arthur's knight has failed. But, my young squire, perhaps we can use this situation to benefit your education. Tell me what you know of the gwillion."

Mordred sighed, sick of this sort of mental exercise that Gawain preferred. It always required him to put on a tedious display to prove his knowledge, and no matter how thorough, Gawain always found some asinine detail to render his responses lacking. "Gwillion, he began, "are magical beings with certain inherent characteristics. First, they are usually green or gray and between six and eight feet in height. Second, their spindly, overlong arms and legs possess unnatural strength. Third, their black nails, given the time, are hard enough to work through my chainmail shirt. . ." he stopped. "Do we *have* to do this?"

Gawain's mouth curled into an involuntary, good-natured smile, then he forced it back to a line. "Mordred, when I agreed to accept you as my squire, I made a vow to see to your instruction. For a knight of the Round Table, that vow encompasses a number of disciplines, from chivalry, to manners, diplomacy, leadership, fighting, riding, geography, heraldry, modern languages. . . and, most certainly, monsters. Now, you left out the three most important elements—"

"I suppose I should thank you for accepting me," Mordred interrupted, somewhat bitterly. "Everyone else, my *father* included, seems to view me as an abomination, to be avoided. To embrace my birthright and become a great knight, or king, seems to me to be problematic at best."

"One rung at a time, little *brother*," Gawain chided. "Your ambition" here he glanced sideways at his protégé, a conspiratorial smile in his eyes, "is perhaps your *best* attribute. It is a *strength* that pushes you to learn fast, work hard, and improve, but patience, too, is a knightly virtue, necessary to sustained success. You are yet a squire. No knight looks up to a squire, no matter who his father or mother may be." He cleared his throat, consciously avoiding the topic of Mordred's incestuous birth. Someday, he told himself, he would explain that Arthur's aversion to Mordred had more to do with Arthur than Mordred. The boy was a painful reminder of the king's flaws. He was ashamed of himself, not of his son. Sometimes, though, it's as hard for a proud man to admit that as it is for a youth to see past his own self-absorption.

Gawain continued, "Now, as I was saying, three essentials of gwillion: One, you must remember that gwyll flesh heals at an alarming rate—dead gwillion will revivify given time, and severed limbs will conjoin, or even regrow into a new gwyll. Two, though they lack physical eyes (having instead only hollow sockets) gwillion can perceive perfectly in darkness. Merlin speculates that they see not what we see—the world as it is—but rather they *see*' with a satanic vision that seeks out heat and fire. They see, he says, the network of hot blood boiling through our veins. How this can be, I cannot say, but their world is a hellscape. Third—"

"Third, gwillion flesh burns like a torch when kindled, probably because the flames are dragging them back to perdition," Mordred finished in a singsong. "I *know*, brother."

They descended the hill into the pine forest, leaving the blazing sun behind them and riding into shadow. The coolness of the change was a physical relief. Mordred continued, "Here's something you may not, though: I was talking with Aunt Morgana, and she said that all gwillion are really just *one* gwyll—that's why they're all female. Apparently, the first was conjured long ago by a rogue druid, right here, she said, on Anglesey. The gwyll was the druid's minion, and when he was hunted and killed by the first king of Gwynedd, they chopped up the gwyll and scattered it to the four winds. Each bit—each thigh, forearm, and finger—then grew into a separate gwyll, and thus the race was born.²"

"I wish you wouldn't speak to our aunt so much. She's deceitful and

---

² Because some of you may not possess an accurate knowledge of Welsh folklore, a clarification: gwyll (pluralized gwyllion) is a Welsh word that most directly translates into "darkness" or "gloom." The gwyll itself is immortalized in Welsh stories—most frequently as a "boogieman" to scare children—but has interestingly taken many shapes over the ages. Like the Norse "trolls," which can vary in tales from lumbering, ogre-esque giants of questionable intelligence, to hideous green-skinned bog-dwelling terrors, even to ugly dwarfish children of mischievous intent, gwyllion have had many manifestations: fey elven women, hideous hags, monstrous midnight stalkers, or shadows that inhabit the body and bring nightmares. Invariably, though they are female beings of faerie, associated with mountains, woods, darkness, and nightfall.

scheming. Believe me, to her you are but a pawn in some grandiose strategy." He rubbed his close-cropped beard. "Tell me, did you get all this nonsense about strength and weakness from her?"

"Certainly not," Mordred replied, offended. "I am quite capable of having my own ideas."

A red squirrel with comically tufted ears chittered down at them from a treetop. A horse could be heard, whinnying, ahead.

"Ah," Gawain nodded, changing the subject, "Edgar reports."

Sure enough, the smallish yeoman appeared, trotting through the tall columns of pine. The wood was thick with trees, living and dead, but despite this, the understory gave the impression of airy openness. There was little undergrowth and the green branches of the pines began a dozen or more feet in the air, providing a roof of living needles and a carpet of dead ones, the space between pillared by myriad reddish-gray trunks.

Edgar, the forester, trotted closer, his tanned skin nearly indiscernible from his leather garments. A quiver of goose-fletched arrows jostled on one flank of his horse, and a round metal shield on the other. Across his back was slung a yew-wood bow, and a carved hunting horn thumped against his ribs. He pulled up a few paces from Gawain and his morose brown eyes came to rest on his lord's face.

"Over that rise," he gestured behind him, "the gwyll-sign begins. Bones of deer and sheep, scarred trees, the acid stench of its foul piss. Even the forest is dying. We're entering the thing's lair, certain."

"How long until we catch it?" Gawain asked.

Edgar turned his weathered face to the yellowing sky. He spat. "Nightfall, I'd guess."

"Not an ideal time for a gwyll-fight, sir," a deep voice warned. Gawain's two purple-clad men at arms caught up, halting a pace or two behind their leader.

"Indeed, not, Brom," Gawain responded, nodding at the younger and burlier of the two, "but we daren't wait for daylight to transact our business." Privately, he admitted to himself, he agreed with Brom. It would certainly be better to take the gwyll during daylight, but given the captive Margaret, he wasn't in a position to delay. Regretfully, he acknowledged the likelihood of losing one or more of his men tonight.

For his part, Brom only nodded in terse agreement.

"We all know the plan?" Gawain asked. "Edgar, find it for us. Alert us with your horn. We'll be right behind. Brom, you and I will face it in combat. You keep it at bay with a boar-spear and I'll use my axe to dismember it."

Brom nodded again.

Gawain then considered the older man at arms, a kindly faced, thin-bearded fellow of forty. He was well past his prime, Gawain thought, but a loyal man, tactful and observant. He seemed an ideal choice for a diplomatic trip to Anglesey. Now he'd be endangered, too. No time for that, though. "Erving, you and Mordred kindle a fire with the wood on the packhorse, then feed the flames and keep them burning. You've the pitchfork?"

"Yes, sir," Erving responded, "It's tied to the brush on the pony."

"Good. Once the fire is lit, skewer any dismembered gwyll parts—careful. They'll be squirming; the hands will still claw at you—and cook them in the flame."

He turned to Edgar, "While we fight, rescue the girl. She's young, just twelve years. She'll be terrified."

Edgar nodded.

"Anything else," Gawain asked.

"One thing, sir," Edgar ventured. "Not sure if it matters, but I should report it. Twice now I've seen a strange beast, a white deer, in the woods. It examined me. . ." he hesitated. "Not like a deer, but like a man. I think, well," he hesitated. "I think it may be following us."

Gawain shot Mordred a look. "Thoughts?"

"A druid, maybe?" Mordred offered. "This isle was their sanctuary in ages past. It would explain why the gwyll is acting abnormally, if it's under a spell and following orders. Edgar, was it a stag or doe?"

Edgar looked to Gawain before answering. Gawain noted the man's reluctance to make eye contact with Mordred or treat him with respect—something he'd have to remedy, but now wasn't the time.

"Well?" Gawain asked.

"Hard to say—it was strange, lacking all markings and distinctions. No antlers, though. A doe, I suppose."

Mordred rubbed his nose, thoughtful. "Odd. Druids are male."

Gawain sighed. Indeed, he thought, it was strange, and, yet, as much as he hated to proceed on a dangerous mission with uncertainties multiplying around him, he saw little choice but to move forward. "It may just be a white deer," he concluded. "We don't have time to worry about it now or alter the plan. Edgar, if you see it again, shoot it. Now let's get to business. Don your helms, check your straps and buckles. Ready your weapons. We've got a gwyll to kill."

The gathering broke up. Edgar trotted off in front, Gawain followed, tall in the saddle on Gringolet; his polished helm and white steed were lights in the gathering shadow. Mordred trailed him, tightening the straps of his shoulder plates, the only armor he wore over his chainmail shirt. Behind them rode Brom and Erving, spears in hand and leading the heavily-laden packhorse. They rode into the dell and up the next hill, cresting it and disappearing from view.

Shadowing them, out of sight and silent on the carpet of soft brown needles, trotted a white doe. Behind it, out past the forest, the cliff, and the ribbed, sandy beach, the orange sun sank into the churning waters of the Irish Sea.

***

After cresting the hill, they wound into a twisting valley, at the bottom of which lay a dry stream. The bed was gray, littered with broken shards of slate, the edges polished smooth by the spring rains. Here and there a small pool lay in a low spot. On the valley walls, raggedly striated bands of rock poked out at intervals in cliffs and smaller formations. Occasionally, these had collapsed into rockslides of shifting stone, dangerous for the horses to cross, requiring the party to dismount and walk. Twilight began to fade around them.

"There's another one, sir" Erving gestured left, and, sure enough, bright white bone shone through the gathering gloom: a series of ribs, large, like a cow.

"Hold," Mordred ordered.

Gawain reined in, curious.

"That's not like the others." Mordred said. He dismounted, landing softly in the needles then coughing, as the thick, biting stench of uric acid curled up from the forest floor, the creature's excrement. The nearest pine tree was dead. Bark flaked and curled off the trunk. When he rested his hand upon it, Mordred could feel the shallow channels, wheeling scars left by bark-eating beetles. He walked over, disinterring the creature's skull from a pile of needles and flat rocks. It was large and thick with an oversized nasal cavity and inch-long canine teeth. Mordred kicked the needles, sending both stones and curved brownish claws scattering.

"Well?" Gawain asked. Mordred handed the skull up to him before remounting.

"A bear. A large one, clearly the old king of these woods." He settled into the saddle. "That must have been quite a contest."

The closer that they got to the gwyll's lair, the more numerous the skeletons became, mostly of deer, sheep, and other harmless animals, but there were some human remains mixed in, too. Earlier, Mordred's gelding had mistakenly trod upon half a cranium. It shattered like a dry gourd. This bear, however, was the first evidence of a large predator that they'd seen. Mordred's eyes watered from the acrid stench. He rubbed them and scanned the area, almost certain that he was being watched. Nothing moved.

Following a quick examination, Gawain discarded the skull. It struck the ground with a crack, and the jawbone fell out, tumbling into the streambed. He looked into the fading amethyst of the sky. Two twinkling stars were now visible. Shaking his head, he put a knee into Gringolet's flank and rode ahead, silent and contemplative. Erving came forward, matching speed with Mordred. He eyed the skull for a moment, then spoke, nervous.

"We'll be working together."

"So it would seem," Mordred replied.

"You want the pitchfork or the fire?"

"I'll use the fork."

"Alright. Good. I just want you to know, um. . ." Erving hesitated, unsure of the proper form of address for a squire of high birth, ". . .*Sir*, that I'm happy to work with you. A lot of folks talk. They judge you based on your birth, but not me." His conversation picked up pace and confidence as he went. "Seems to me you can't blame a man for the decisions of his parents or who they are. That's out of a man's control. My father taught me that. See, I'm not his son, but he took me in 'cause he couldn't have none of his own. Without his kindness I'd be nothing. Dead, likely." He smiled "So, sir, you had some bad luck, maybe. But I tell you this: I serve Lady Morgause, and my father—one of King Lot's men—did before me, and she's a fine, kind, loyal, lady. And I've admired your father all my life. Anyone would be lucky to be his son. So," he hesitated again, then brought his long ramble to a close, "any son of theirs would be a man I'm eager to follow."

Mordred watched Erving's face carefully. He nodded, noncommittal.

"And, begging your pardon if I'm asking too bold, sir, but one day I'd be happy to be in your service." His coarse white cheeks reddened.

In response, Mordred softened his expression and clapped a hand on Erving's shoulder. "And you shall be of great service, friend. I'll need men of loyalty at my side." He nodded again, coughed, and spat. "Thank you."

They rode up the silent valley: no birds, no squirrel chatter, nothing but the breeze moaning through tall pines overhead, the creaking groans of straining red-barked trunks, and the clatter of hoofbeats echoing off rock faces. His horse sidestepped a discarded axe, its blade rusted and handle rotten from one or more winters, exposed in the streambed. Mordred turned to Erving to ask a question, but as he did, the silence was torn by the sound of a hunting horn, not far ahead. The long, loud blast was followed by a succession of staccato notes, moving toward them along the defile, somewhere over the ridge.[3]

---

[3] The hunting horn, which (as the name suggests) was originally carved from an animal horn—in this case from a bull—was a crude instrument capable of only one pitch, and the note that could be played was determined by the length and diameter of the horn in question. Rather than attempting to vary the pitch, early hunters varied the length of their blowing to produce different effects. This was used to create a sort of early hunter's code. In this case, Edgar's initial blast was a signal that the quarry had been spotted, and the following short bursts were an appeal for haste.

"Forward, lads," Gawain called, kneeing his stallion and picking up the pace, but carefully, still, because of the treacherous footing. Brom followed, passing by Mordred. The horn sounded again, more desperate, then fell silent.

"Onward, man!" Mordred ordered Erving, urging his gelding along and into the wake of sliding slate scattered behind the leaders.

A pair of horrible, high-pitched growls, ending in throaty gurgles, sounded down the valley. The noise bristled the hair on Mordred's neck and set his teeth on edge. Goosebumps rippled down his arms. His horse faltered then regained his footing. Mordred squinted ahead. The gwillion snarled again, less simultaneous this time. The sounds came from over the nearest rise, only a handful of minutes away. Mordred's gelding pulled up.

"Two?!" Erving called. "There are two of them?"

"Two at least," Mordred confirmed. Gawain and Brom were nearly at the top now. "No matter," he replied with artificial cheerfulness, "we must carry out the plan. Others are relying on us. Onward." He resumed his ascent, determined to show himself to be a knight of valor equaling his brother's.

The horn blew again, fast staccatos, much closer and yet more desperate.

Gawain pulled up at the top of the incline, unlooping a large two-handed battleaxe from his saddle.

A scream rent the dusky air, not the beasts', and not the scream of death—not yet—it was a battle cry, the kind of desperate wailing growl uttered by cornered animals, but on this occasion from a man.

Gawain dismounted, abandoning Gringolet, and disappearing over the rise. Brom leapt from his mount and followed suit, spear in hand.

Over the clatter of hooves, Mordred heard a series of sharp hissing wails, clearly a gwyll in pain, then Edgar howled in terror and agony, the visceral noise modulated into a gurgle, then silenced.

Mordred crested the rise. "Christ," he exclaimed.

Ahead of him the valley lowered slightly. A snag, a tangle of toppled trees, chest-high and bristling with piercing, odd-angle branches, stood between him and a twenty-foot cliff, looming fifty yards beyond. After a rain, water would surely cascade down its stone face. Now, though, only some damp moss and a small stagnant pool remained, carved by the spring waters into an empty basin. On the far shore of the pool, the silhouette of a creature loomed in the darkness. Yet, this was no normal gwyll. The eight-foot, lanky monster had two heads on her shoulders, each crowned with short twisting antlers. Three white glints in the darkness indicated goose-fletched arrows protruding from her torso, but to no avail. She bent down, the shapely outlines of her breasts visible against the cliff, and tore into something. There was a ripping of flesh and popping of tendons. A bone snapped audibly, echoing off the cliff. With a shiver, Mordred realized that it must be Edgar's.[4]

Branches broke to Mordred's left, shifting his attention. Gawain and Brom pushed through the snag, rushing, too late, to the aid of their slain fellow. Mordred turned to Erving. "Can we take the packhorse around?" He scanned the area to the right, seeing snag all the way to an impossibly high hill, crowned with broken stumps, clearly impassable by a horse.

"No, sir," Erving answered. "But perhaps we can carry it through, afoot." He gestured to a steep path leading up and over an outcrop, hidden in the brush. "It'll be hard, but with both of us, we may be able to make it. The wood's bundled tight."

"Good," Mordred moved toward the horse. "Be sure you bring your flint. The load is secured to the harness. Let's take that. It will be faster than rebundling it."

Gawain leapt down from the last log in the snag, his great-helm knocking against his head. Through the constricting vision of its slit, he focused on the two-headed gwyll, feeding on Edgar. Brom landed with a grunt beside him.

"Careful now," Gawain's muffled voice cautioned through the faceplate. "Edgar's dead, so we needn't charge in, heedless. Can you spot the girl?"

"There's something back behind it, certain." Brom said. "A lump of cloth, not moving. It's big enough to be the young lady."

They edged toward the gwyll. "We'll assume it's her," Gawain said. "Remember, keeping her safe is our priority." He glanced back. "It will take time for Mordred and Erving to carry the wood through that snag. We'll be on our own for a while. Nothing hasty; delay, maneuver—we'll try to get between the beast and the girl. Remember, your role is defensive. The spear stays between us and the creature, keeping it back. I've got the axe. I need room to do the cutter's work." He realized that he was talking more for his

---

[4] A two-headed gwyll, you may ask, how can that possibly be? Well, in this particular case, the deformity happened to have been caused by a brave warrior wielding a bastard or hand-and-a-half sword (the warrior—Cadfael by name—is now dead, of course). In a previous encounter, this brave and enterprising Welshman ambushed the gwyll, leaping from a tree and bringing his blade down on her with mortal force. The bright blade cleaved the gwyll's head in two from crown down through the neck, and even slightly into the chest. Obviously, the rest of the conflict didn't go as well for the Welshman. Afterwards, however, as the gwyll recovered, each head healed separately, resulting in the peculiar mutation of our current adversary.

own benefit, to calm his nerves, so he bit his lip, advancing toward the creature.

One of the gwyll's heads stopped feeding, lifting to watch them while the other tore out Edgar's intestines, swallowing them in a series of jerking gulps, until they finally ripped free from the excoriated belly. The creature was still bathed in shadow. Its feminine outline could be clearly seen, long spindly arms, folded legs, prominent breasts. One arm reached up and snapped off each of the protruding arrows in succession, tossing them into the nearby pool, were they floated, fletches white against the dark water. The still-chewing head stared idly in their direction.

His sight hampered by the helm, Gawain inadvertently trod upon what he assumed was a branch (it was a rib). It cracked, and the gwyll rose, claws flexing at its sides. Both heads focused on the approaching warriors. One cocked to the side; the other snarled, a low-pitched warning. Gawain halted, cautious.

The gwyll advanced a step.

The warriors held their ground.

In response, both heads roared. A horrible stunning sound—twinned, repeated, overlapping, echoing—erupted from the creature and she charged with remarkable speed and agility, scattering stones as she came.

Gawain's axe came up. Brom set his spear, bracing it into the earth and against his boot, leaning in and expecting impact. None came.

The gwyll stopped—incredible that she could halt from a full sprint—a pace from the spear, and batted it out of the way with an offhand swing. She lunged in for a kill, only to be met by Gawain's axe, which cut a trailing scar down her chest, three-inches deep from shoulder to naval, splitting the right breast in two.

The monster wailed, retreating. Steaming ichor bubbled from the wound, which was already healing before their eyes. Brom stabbed in, jabbing the spear into her armpit, leaving a second bubbling wound.

"Brom," Gawain shouted. "Stay defensive. With me, now." Gawain moved left, still working to maneuver between the creature and the girl, but Brom hesitated. The gwyll sprang, landing between the two warriors, her back to the great knight.

Terrified, Brom lunged. The spear struck the monster with remarkable force. Its steel head penetrated her chest, lifting her off the ground, pushing her back, and protruding an inch through her shoulder, the wood shaft lodged into what should have been the monster's heart. She was rammed back into Gawain, who stumbled, lacking room to wield his cumbersome axe. He recovered his footing, ready to strike, but it was already too late.

The gwyll pounced and Brom screamed. She seized his arms, wrenching them in opposite directions. Both of the eyeless heads struck at

Brom's neck from opposing sides. His scream intensified. Flesh split, tendons snapped and popped, and his arms tore free, flinging out to the gwyll's sides. One was plucked out at the shoulder and the other twisted off at the elbow. The former pinwheeled into the cliff, and the latter splashed out into the pool. Blood rained into the clearing. Brom, and his scream, died.

Gawain's axe came down on the gwyll's left arm as it arced up. At the midpoint between the upper elbow and shoulder, the perfectly honed steel made contact.[5] The greenish skin resisted, briefly, but the blade sang, slashing through one side and out the other, then down to split a large slate. The severed arm dropped, thrashing, to the earth, and the gwyll's heads released their victim.

Brom's body toppled backwards, armless, landing chest-up on a pile of scattered stone. His head lolled to the side, connected to the torso only by an exposed, bloody spine. The rest of his neck was gone, devoured. Gawain retreated, now in a defensive stance. Behind his expressionless helm, his face was pale and terrified. Sweat dripped from his nose. The gwyll rounded on him, her one remaining arm wrenching the spear from her chest.

High above, atop the cliff, the white doe observed the scene, impassive. It could see Gawain backpedaling as the gwyll advanced, regaining strength as her wounds closed and healed. The monster roared and the knight flinched. Behind the creature, the Welsh girl crawled along the cliff wall toward the snag, hoping, no doubt, to escape, but she was oblivious to the severed arm that writhed and clawed steadily closer along the uneven ground. Near the pool's edge, Mordred was busy stacking wood in a pile, while the only remaining man at arms was frantically striking flint on steel to kindle the flame. A wisp smoke rose from where he crouched.

The gwyll discarded the spear and advanced, heedless of danger. She flailed at Gawain, tearing his surcoat and rending four curling tracks into the steel of his breastplate, but catching no flesh. Gawain reeled and reset his feet. The monster lunged again, striking at his head, but he struck, too, bringing his axe in sideways with all the force that his broad frame and musclebound arms could muster.

The gwyll's arm and Gawain's axe made simultaneous contact from opposite sides. The gwyll's palm slammed into Gawain's helm as his bright axe bit into one of her necks. The axe traveled through, severing a head,

---

[5] Yes, you read that right. In fact, gwyllion have twin-jointed arms and legs (each joint bends opposite from the other), allowing them increased flexibility and mobility compared to humans. In one of us, of course, this kind of multi-joint arrangement would be a great disadvantage; most human injuries occur at the intersections of bones. Yet, in a creature with the magical restorative powers of the gwyllion, this only amplified their abilities.

which fell, still snarling, to earth. But Gawain, too, was falling. The contact twisted and removed his helm, lifted him off his feet, and sent him cartwheeling through the air to slam, face first, into the uneven surface of the slate wall. He crumpled, concussed, bleeding, and unable to move. His axe clattered at the creature's feet. A horrible metallic groan sounded as she crushed and dropped the helm. Then bending, she picked the weapon up, stared at it briefly, and tossed it into the pool. It splashed, vanishing beneath the surface.

Mordred's fire burst into brilliant, crackling life, illuminating the rocky basin. The gwyll turned to face it and for the first time became fully visible. A dark seaweed green, with lighter, grayish marks where wounds had healed, she was a nightmarish figure in the flickering firelight, even bloodied and butchered as she was. Her remaining head was shaped like a poorly-crafted clay model: oblong like an ape's, it had a beak-like but functionless nose, lacking nostrils; deep sockets, lacking eyes; an overlarge, drooping mouth full of serrated black teeth; and no ears at all. The short antlers protruding from her temples had the haphazardly contorting shape and gray texture of tree-roots. The gwyll was hairless, but covered in a thick skin that seemed something akin to beech-bark, and a bulging network of veins or tendons ran shallowly, pulsating beneath it. Her chest was large, though not visibly drawing breath. Two swelling breasts protruded, absent of nipples. The gwyll's long, spindle arm was dual-jointed, and the claws on its hand were easily three inches in length and serrated like her teeth. Looking closely, Mordred could see the skin boiling along the lines of her injuries, fleshy tendrils forming, wrapping, joining, tightening; already, Gawain's long axe-cut was mostly healed.

Mordred stared down the gwyll, his fingers nervously twitching against the handle of the pitchfork, clutched firmly in both hands. He felt hopelessly exposed in his chainmail shirt and open-faced helm, and hopelessly outmatched in his fifteen-year-old body. Beside him, the fire doubled in intensity as Erving frantically fed it dry branches from the snag, and in the increased light, Mordred caught sight of a white figure standing atop the nearest cliff. No longer a doe, she was a middle-aged woman wearing a pale gown. Clearly recognizable—even from that distance—was his aunt, Morgana.

The gwyll turned, advancing on Gawain's unconscious body. Not far from him, the girl began to scream, confronted with the severed arm. Mordred looked to her, inexplicably torn between the decision to run to her rescue or to aid Gawain, but he only faltered for a moment, then he launched himself at the creature, arriving just as she began to close on his brother.

Gawain opened his eyes, licking blood from his lips, and blinking in confusion. Directly above him, a blurry figure dressed in white seemed to float atop the cliff. To his side, backlit against an orange blaze of fire, a dark silhouette brandishing a wicked, four-pronged pitchfork advanced violently. Uncomprehending, his mind briefly considered the possibility that he was dead, that his soul lay balanced between an angel and a devil: heaven and hell, but then a terrible growl snapped him from his reverie and he remembered the gwyll.

She advanced, lurching lopsidedly (missing both left arm and head). Gawain fumbled for his sword, already aware that he'd be too late. As her terrible jaws lowered toward him, however, the gwyll was thrown sideways into the cliff wall. Mordred's pitchfork was deep in her chest, pinning her in place.

"Kill it!" Mordred screamed, but there was another, more terrified screaming too, close along the cliff wall. Margaret, Gawain realized. In abject terror, the girl kicked and struggled, with something wrapped around her throat.

"Kill it!" Mordred ordered, again, but Gawain was indecisive. He stood frozen for a moment, sword out, salty and iron-bitter blood streaming from his broken nose, through his blonde goatee, and dribbling off his chin.

The girl's scream rose in pitch, and then smothered, turning to painful and hopeless gurgled sobbing. The gwyll snarled at Mordred, shoving at him, using the cliff as leverage. With a massive effort, he slammed her back into the wall, and then Gawain made his choice.

"Pin it there!" the knight shouted, as he turned, rushing to save young Margaret.

The gwyll lashed out at Mordred with her arm, the claws raking his mail shirt, rending it and slicing shallowly across the boy's stomach. Steel rings showered the ground, pinging off at wild angles. Mordred leapt back, stumbled, his fall wrenching the pitchfork free. The gwyll stood over him. Mordred inhaled, the realization of his inevitable death a revelation to him. He would, he reasoned, die here because Gawain chose a worthless girl over his own flesh and blood—over his own brother. He spat out one last word, full of derision: "*Chivalry.*"

The gwyll's clawed arm lifted, poised to come down, ending his life. But Erving arrived at that moment. He slammed, bodily, into the monster, knocking her back a pace, then he brought his sword down in an arc, seemingly to slash the beast in the chest, but he held the blade, stopping the momentum. There, fixed upon end of the longsword's bright blade was the gwyll's severed head, alight and burning like it had been soaked in pitch.

The creature backed away from the flames and Erving advanced, the sizzling head held between them. Its gaping mouth yawned, forming a voiceless scream. Droplets of flaming ichor fell from it at intervals, hissing as they hit the cool stones. Mordred rose, his pitchfork at the ready.

Erving thrust the blazing head into the gwyll's abdomen and the monster combusted, engulfed in roaring flame. Thick, acrid smoke curled into the night sky. The creature screamed in terror and pain, lashing her claw at the man at arms. Erving grunted and fell, tossed aside like Gawain before him. He bled from three parallel gashes in one bicep. Clutching his wound, he scrabbled backwards until his back was against the cliff.

The gwyll turned toward the pool of water in the rocky basin, but Mordred was prepared. He thrust the pitchfork into her again, calling over his shoulder to Gawain. "Help me, brother!"

The gwyll grabbed the fork's shaft with her burning claw, dragging herself and Mordred toward the water, but she never got there.

Unobserved by the warriors, Morgana had descended the cliff and now stood firmly on the stone floor of the basin. She smiled benignly, held two crooked hands before her, spread her fingers, and touched her thumbs together. Her lips mouthed the word, "Llosg," and a conical jet of pallid blue flame burst forth, enveloping the gwyll, whose scream shifted in tenor from terrifying to terrified. Mordred fell back from the heat of the blaze, momentarily blinded by the light. The creature simply ceased to exist.[6]

Morgana cut off her flames, and the basin darkened, now lit only by the wan flame of Erving's comparatively anemic bonfire. Gawain stood over Mordred, sword drawn.

"Erving," he ordered, not looking at his man. The girl is hurt. Bind her wounds. He offered Mordred a hand up. "Unharmed?"

"Mere scratches," Mordred answered, taking Gawain's hand, then gesturing to his abdomen.

Gawain returned his attention to the witch, Morgan le Fay. "What do you want with us, *aunt?*" he asked, his tone acid.

She smiled. "Is this the thanks you owe to the woman who saved your lives, or is it——rather——the duty owed to a beloved aunt? I cannot tell. In either case, I cringe at your lack of chivalry."

"I suspect," Gawain replied, "that this——" he gestured around the basin "——is all your doing. Congratulations, *dearest* aunt; you have saved me from yourself."

Morgana's smile faded. "You always were a fool, Gawain. But my business is not with you, not *yet*, in any case." She turned to Mordred. "Your brother is right, this was all for your benefit, and it progressed exactly as I knew it would."

"Go on," Mordred said.

"My nephew is so pedantically predictable. My gwyll stole a girl. The 'great hero' came to save her. I offered him a choice of her life or yours, and

---

[6] In case you don't know Welsh, the word "llosg" is a verb most nearly meaning "incinerate."

he showed you the way he values family by choosing her—don't worry, *I* wouldn't have let it happen, in any case. I *do* care about my family," she turned toward Gawain, "which is the *only* reason that you are still alive." Then, looking back to Mordred, "He doesn't value you, dear nephew. None of them do, not like your aunt, Morgana, does. I've come to offer you a choice, an opportunity."

"He's already made his choice," Gawain interrupted. Morgana flipped her hand in his direction and he toppled, knocked off his feet by some invisible force.

"We'll let *him* make it, I think," she said.

"What is my choice, aunt?" Mordred asked, advancing a step toward her.

"To stay with him," she gestured at Gawain as he struggled to his feet, playfully knocking him back down, "or to come with me. You see, Mordred, you have a power in you, ancient as the hills and rocks—the same power that flows through me. I shall instruct you in its secrets, help you to unlock it. You shall be a warlock, a wizard to vie with Merlin!"

Mordred stared at her, his mouth curling into a pleased smirk.

"Think of it!" she continued, "the power to control the elements, to shape minds, to bestow pleasure or inflict pain; it will be yours. You will be the greatest man in Britain!" She paused, expectant. Mordred considered. "It is your birthright and your destiny," she urged.

"Aunt," Mordred replied. "While my spirit surely yearns for the power that you offer, I find that I must refuse."

Surprise and then confused dismay flashed across Morgana's face.

"I have," Mordred explained, "recently observed that my greatest strength is my ambition, and I would hate to allow it to also be my downfall." He offered a hand to Gawain, raising him up. They made eye contact and nodded. Then Mordred looked back to his aunt. "*Patience*," he laid emphasis on the word, "is a knightly virtue, and I find that I am inclined to be a knight, after all."

Morgana's confused expression was rapidly changing to one of annoyance.

"I'm sorry to have put you to all this trouble," Mordred added, gesturing to the carnage around the hollow basin, sarcasm clearly apparent in his tone. "Had you simply asked me earlier, I might have saved you the effort."

In response, Morgana advanced a step, becoming visibly angry. "You refuse me? A fifteen-year-old boy?!"

"Was I incorrect in assuming that you meant it when you offered me a *choice*?" Mordred asked. "Or do you intend to seize me, regardless of my wish? You are capable of doing so, of course; I'd be a fool to dispute your power."

"Indeed you would," Morgana agreed, "and perhaps I will."

"You'll seize him over my corpse, then" Gawain said, grimly, raising his sword and stepping between Mordred and his aunt. "I'll die for him, gladly."

"It seems you shall," Morgana agreed, "and it will be a great pleasure to me." She spread her hands again.

Thinking quickly, Mordred withdrew a bit, inverted his pitchfork and brought a full swing against the back of Gawain's skull. The wood connected with a resounding crack and Gawain crumpled (again) to the ground. Morgana lowered her arms, befuddled.

"I'd rather you didn't," Mordred explained. "Now it's my turn to talk, *aunt*, if you'll promise to listen."

She nodded, intrigued.

"I could tell this was your doing from the moment Gruffudd sent us on this ridiculous chase. I watched Gawain walking into the jaws of your baited trap——so predictably, too."

"And yet," she interrupted, "you choose to follow him?"

"I choose power," Mordred responded, "just as I always will. My ambition makes me predictable, perhaps. You certainly calculated on that. But, it need not be so if I struggle against it. When Gawain awakes, I will leave this place with him, and in a moment, I will explain my reasoning to you, and you will agree with me. Erving!" he called over his shoulder, "how is young Margaret?"

"Unconscious" he replied, "but breathing and bandaged. She'll live, I believe." The man at arms walked closer, staring at Gawain's felled form. "Why, sir, did you...?" he trailed off.

"To save his life," Mordred responded. "Your arm bleeds. See to it," he ordered.

Erving knelt, tearing a strip from his cloak.

To his aunt, Mordred said, "Now, Aunt Morgana, I owe you an explanation. I choose *lasting* power. What you offer me is tempting because it is easy and immediate, but we both know that it won't win in the end. You, aunt, can conquer any*one* with magic, but you cannot defeat Arthur. Why? Because he is not *one*. He rules because he leads and others follow——tens of thousands of others. They follow because he is a great man, and his greatness comes from his good nature, his virtue. Certainly, that is a weakness that I (and hopefully you, as well) will soon exploit to his downfall, but it is undeniably the root of his strength. Hold——one moment." Here Mordred paused, turning to Erving, who was staring at him with wonder.

"Sir?" Erving asked, rising to his feet and obviously unsure how to respond to what he just heard.

Without visible hesitation, Mordred rammed the pitchfork into the man's chest, all four tines driving home. The blow forced Erving back and onto his knees.

"Oh," he said with a touch of sullenness. He ran a calloused finger down the fork's handle, gurgled, and toppled to his side, his fading eyes fixed on Mordred's face. Even Morgana was taken aback.

"Before we continued this discussion," Mordred said, instructionally, "I needed to prove to you that I am both intelligent and in earnest. I had two problems. Both are now solved. Gawain will soon wake, wondering who hit him, and Erving, here," he gestured at his fallen fellow "was overhearing a conversation that I must keep secret. So, it appears that Erving was working for you, snuck up behind us, and clubbed Gawain, a treachery for which I *silenced* him," he turned and watched as Erving's lips tried to form a word, blood trickling from his mouth, "forever."

Morgana nodded. "Continue, nephew."

"As I said, Arthur's virtue is his strength because it earns him loyalty, and as long as he has that, he is never alone. *That*, my dear aunt, I've come to realize, is the root of lasting earthly power. If I did as you suggest and became a grand wizard, I might indeed be powerful. I would certainly inspire fear and command respect, but it would be in vain—illegitimately forced on my subjects and followers alike. Their jealousy and hatred would simmer beneath the surface. Ultimately, in a moment of weakness, I would fail, just as you have always done." He held up a hand and shushed her. "Deny it if you like, but it rings true, nonetheless. You've failed, aunt, time and again, and I think, perhaps, the day is come that you'll agree to cede command of your enterprise to a new general."

Morgana sneered. "You? A mere boy?"

"Yes," Mordred replied, bluntly. He tore the pitchfork from Erving's corpse and planted its butt-end on the ground beside him. "Consider: Arthur can only be defeated from within. He can only be broken by losing his virtue. That is where I shall strike him, and I will be most patient in my planning, as I was today. Yes, one day I will skin my father's virtue, his goodness, off of him and drape it upon my own shoulders as a king dons a resplendent cloak. And that day, my dear aunt, your revenge will *finally* be complete."

Morgana smiled, impressed. "You will need my advice in this venture, if you are to succeed," she began.

Mordred scoffed, "Your advice? Perhaps you successfully anticipated Gawain's every move, but you did not foresee mine. It was, rather, I who predicted yours. And I continue to do so. Let me be plain: you, Gawain, and I are all here at *my* bidding. From the first, this has been my plan (though I admit that your gwyll was an inspired addition). I planted the seed of this in your mind at our last meeting. Yes, that's right—on the equinox—you remember. But I'm a youth, you say? Yes, fifteen years old and unaided, vying with a powerful king, confident in my ultimate victory. What's more, when I leave this place, I will have your allegiance—necessary for me to contend with

Arthur and counter Merlin—and I will have shown myself to be the most promising young warrior in Camelot, and *loyal* enough to earn the mighty Gawain's trust and sponsorship. I will be admired by all and knighted early, and so I will move closer to *our* goal."

Gawain groaned, shifting slightly.

Mordred glanced down, then locked his aunt in a dark-eyed stare. "All that remains is for you to openly acknowledge my supremacy."

"And if so, what then will I do?" Morgana asked, pale eyes resting on her nephew with a newfound respect, and—perhaps—even cautious subservience.

"You will depart, leaving us unharmed, and you will wait for my next instructions. As you go, you shall consider all of my words, and—undoubtedly—you will question if they are true, if I mean them or if I am playing you for a fool. The query is, in point of fact, rhetorical. Nevertheless, you will, in your pride, certainly consider returning here to kill us both. However, if I am as clever as we both suspect that I am, you will have no choice but to trust me. For my part, I will rely upon you, aunt, because my path to the throne (and your path to revenge) is much shorter if we are allies."

"You've said all now?"

"All. Make your choice."

Gawain groaned again, his hand moving fractionally toward his head.

"My nephew wakes," Morgana observed (to which nephew she referred was anyone's guess). "I shall leave you," she said, "and shall consider your words. We will speak again on this topic."

Mordred nodded. "If we must. Farewell, aunt."

"Farewell, Mordred," she replied, then turned, hiked up her pale gown, and began picking her way up the hillside, into the darkness. Mordred turned his back on her.

"Up, brother," he grunted, laying down the fork, and straining with the effort of dragging Gawain to the cliff. Mordred propped him into a sitting position. "Rest here a bit," he commanded, "while I clean up the gwyll."

Mordred wandered around the basin, spearing bits of gwyll flesh with the fork and depositing them in the fire. When he reached Margaret, he noted several severed gwyll fingers squirming upon the ground. He picked one up, studied it, then popped it into the pouch on his belt, thinking to himself, who knew what use it could be? He then tossed the remaining fingers, one after another, into the flames. Finally, he turned to Margaret, gently lifted her, and carried her to Gawain, laying her tenderly beside him. He stroked her brown, frizzy hair. "All's well, lass. You'll be home soon," he soothed. His brother smiled wanly up at him.

"Mordred?" Gawain groaned, his eyes trying to focus.

"Right here, brother." Mordred pressed Gawain's hand.

"Our aunt?"

"Gone," Mordred replied. "I changed her mind." He smiled. "She wasn't happy, but she wasn't yet ready to kill me, and she loves you, brother. Yes, deep down she knows it—you're her sister's son."

"As are you," Gawain replied, rubbing his head. "What happened?"

"It's a sad tale," Mordred said. "Erving snuck up behind us and clubbed you. I murdered him for it. The pitchfork was in my hands."

"Erving? He's always been loyal."

"He was mother's man, and Morgana is her sister." Mordred stared at the fire. "Now that I've had time to consider it, though, I think he may have been trying to save you by preventing a fight between you and Morgana. That's why I call my actions murder. Trust me, I regret my quick reaction. I rather liked Erving. He seemed a good man."

Gawain put a calloused hand on Mordred's knee. "It cannot be remedied now. You did what you felt right—what you had to do."

"What I had to do," Mordred agreed. "But now we must get away from this forsaken place and return Margaret to her father. She lives. Can you ride?"

"Gringolet can carry me, whether I can ride or not."

"Rest here," Mordred said. "I'll load the remains of our men on their horses and help carry Margaret out. She can ride with me."

Gawain nodded, his head settling back against the rock. He drifted in and out of sleep while Mordred worked, gathering corpses and weapons and carrying them back through the snag. He returned to move Margaret, then again for his brother.

"Put your arm over my shoulder," Mordred urged. "I'll get you on your horse."

Gawain complied.

"Up," Mordred urged, lifting his brother. Together, Gawain leaning on him for support, they limped toward the snag and their horses. A close observer might have noted that Mordred's belt pouch seemed to be squirming with a will of its own, but in his injured state, Gawain was oblivious.

"How does it feel to have won your first great victory?" Gawain asked as Mordred helped him mount his horse.

Mordred grinned, "Empowering."

***

And here I'll leave you to ponder Mordred's strength and weakness: ambition; Morgana's: revenge; Gawain's: loyalty; and Arthur's: virtue. . . four great figures fated to collide in a legendary conflict, destined to shake and shape the future of a nation.

Scott Davis Howard, an English teacher at Patriot High School in Nokesville, VA, holds an MA in British literature from the University of Montana, Missoula (2008), a BS in communications from Norwich University (2000), is a Washington Post Teacher of the Year nominee, and was a semifinalist in the 2014 Norman Mailer Writing Contest for Educators. He spends his days regaling his 12th grade students with thrilling tales about Beowulf, Sir Gawain, Macbeth, and Dorian Gray, and his nights ferrying his offspring between the soccer field and Cub Scout meetings. In his rare moments of quiet (when the children are munching on snacks in the van, sprinkling crumbs all over the carpet), he wonders when and how he became a soccer mom.

Robert Scott

Business Cards

I hated Mrs. Werner.

Not *Ms.*

Never *Ms.* Werner. She was always and only Mrs. Werner. Although no one had even the first inkling what might have happened to Mr. Werner, back in the 1970s.

I knew.

She'd eaten him, devoured his head like a praying mantis.

Or perhaps her first name was *Mrs.* No rational person could have married that woman on purpose. No way. Not even in *Der Vaterland.* Even Hitler soiled his lederhosen when she assigned homework, "*Eins durch dreißig, bitte. Die underade sind in der Rückseite des Buches.*"

I never said out loud that I hated her, not even after a few beers when a middle-aged dad tends to loosen up around his son, curse a little, reference the salad bar of air-brushed bottoms in the "Victoria's Secret" catalogue. Stuff like that.

But I'd not mentioned my disdain for Mrs. Werner, not even then. I understood what an influential message that would send to Danny.

I disliked her, though, with her nightly practice problems, her seventy-eight-pound textbook, her uncompromising commitment to mathematics above other academic domains.

I wanted to ask if she'd ever read *Huck Finn*, studied the Phoenicians (who were cool), mixed chemicals in a lab, or if she'd just attended the Mathematics Academy for Short Pasty Women of East Berlin. Not kidding: She taught Adolf Hitler, failed his spittle-spraying ass; I'd have bet a month's salary on it.

Just reading her syllabus, I inferred enough to know that Advanced Algebra II was going to run over my son like a frigging snowplow. He'd struggled with Algebra I in ninth grade and worked his ass off to earn a B+ in Geometry. Why they make students sit through a year of shapes class prior to Algebra II will never make sense to me. But then again, I'd not been quite National Honor Society material during my own narrow escape from New Jersey's public school system. So I didn't argue.

And I didn't say anything negative about Mrs. Werner, even though the meticulous, German-engineered efficiency of her syllabus had my back up from the first week of school.

Danny struggled, but he didn't complain. God bless him. He was a better person by seventeen than I'd ever been. I wanted nothing more than to deliver him from Werner's clutches.

So when she failed him on his transformation of functions exam, I offered to meet with her.

Danny shot me down. 'No way, Dad. You'll just make it worse.'

'C'mon, buddy. You were in Connecticut until 8:00 Sunday night.' I pleaded my case. 'You studied in the car. I can vouch for you. It was after midnight when we got home. Of course you were gonna tank. You played in three games Sunday. You were exhausted.'

'No, Dad. Please,' he said, 'lemme talk to her.'

That had been Wednesday morning.

Wednesday night, Danny cried over dinner, embarrassing for a teenage boy in front of his father. She'd summarily turned him down, the club-footed Cyclops, claiming that if he wanted to play travel soccer, he'd have to learn to plan or plan to fail or fail to plan and plan to fail or some appalling figure of speech thousand-year-old teachers use when blowing off otherwise hard working kids.

As my son related this to me, I mentally calculated the odds of falling space junk crushing her to jelly or at least slicing that mole from the end of her nose.

Yeah, all right: She didn't actually have a mole on the end of her nose, but I enjoyed imagining one as I envisioned Skylab plummeting to slice the bulbous end off that vestigial trunk.

Danny cried. He'd been crying too often recently, with my divorce, my wife's relationships around the neighborhood, all of it paraded in front of the judge. Lovely. In her defense, Maggie suggested that I'd been difficult to love, that I had moments of frightening rage, intimidating episodes of nearly blind anger that made it impossible for her to remain faithful to our marriage vows.

But it didn't seem to interfere with her being downright faithful to a number of husbands, friends of friends, even the guy who installed new fixtures in the guest bathroom. (We'll come back to him later.)

Anyway, with Danny's tears fresh in my memory, I called school Thursday morning, was polite, even said 'please' when requesting a time to meet.

At first she wanted to put me off until the next week, claiming that I wouldn't call my doctor or my dentist and expect to get in the next day.

'Actually, Mrs. Werner,' I tried for a chuckle, just to lighten the mood, 'that's exactly when I hope my doctor can fit me in. Because I'm sick . . . you know . . . it's important.'

'So what are you saying, Mr. Edwards?'

I'm saying that you're a cow, a Holstein, but not a cute cow, like at the farmers' fair or on a Chick-fil-A billboard, just a smelly, ugly, pimply, hairy, scabby old cow whose farts destroy the ozone layer and drown all those polar bears in the Arctic.

'I'm saying, Mrs. Werner, that I'd like to get in to see you before the weekend . . . please.'

'8:15 tomorrow, in the office.' She hung up.

I stopped at Starbucks on my way. I had no idea how she took her coffee, if she drank coffee, or if she simply absorbed fluids through her amphibious mucus membranes, the Algebra Teacher from the Black Lagoon. I didn't care. For less than ten dollars I purchased four coffees, each with a different amount of sugar, cream, milk, or sweetener, along a continuum from burned dirt to vanilla frappe. I hoped one might at least be in field goal range of her favorite.

I didn't drink any of them. I'm loyal to Dunkin' Donuts, never developed a taste for burned dirt.

Mrs. Werner didn't drink any of them either, not-so-politely turning me down, as if a parent bringing her a cup of coffee was a gesture tantamount to bribery.

It was. What the hell. So I left the coffee tray in the office. The secretaries looked ready to organize a pep rally in my name.

I wondered if a guidance counselor or an assistant principal might join us, just to referee, but no one did. Mrs. Werner led me into the antiseptic conference room adjacent to the principal's office, sat down, folded her spindly fingers together, and waited for me to plead my case. On the wall behind her, a grumpy bald eagle poster suggested that *Leadership is a Precious Commodity.*

Later, I understood why no one sat in with us: the superintendent of schools, principal, and school board chair could have been in that room encouraging Mrs. Werner to be reasonable, and she would have told them to get bent. Not five minutes into our discussion, I understood that this woman didn't require any assistance putting me in my place.

After ten minutes, I realized that she wasn't about to budge on Danny's failing grade.

At fifteen minutes, I wanted her dead.

By twenty minutes, our discussion had ended and I was fighting back one of those *episodes* my wife's attorney so deftly used against me.

The wheels came off the wagon early:

'It's quite simple, Mr. Edwards; that's my policy. It's clear in my syllabus, which you signed on September ninth. See? Just there.' She slid the signature page across the table.

'I can see that, Mrs. Werner, but please try to understand . . . Danny had three soccer games in New London, Connecticut on Sunday. We didn't get home until after midnight. He tried to study in the car; I promise he did . . . no phone, no music, no tablet, nothing, no video games, just his math book and the review packet, but . . . c'mon . . . he was tired, and –'

'Then maybe you and Mrs. Edwards should rethink your decision to have him playing so much soccer. I've been teaching here for –'

Pissed at her for interrupting, I returned the favor. 'You, Principal Kieffer, the other teachers, college admissions officers, all of you encourage students to be active. Danny plays soccer because he loves it. He loves his coaches and friends, and it's good for him. He's healthy and involved with nice kids. Isn't that what we're supposed to be doing? Keeping him off the couch and out of the Doritos bag?'

'Yet traveling every weekend,' she said. 'I can't slow down the Advanced Algebra curriculum to accommodate year-round soccer. Students, even busy students, have to learn to meet deadlines.'

'He's studied all week,' I tried a different approach. 'He knows the material now.'

'That's very nice, but the test was Monday.'

'So everyone has to learn math at the same time on the same day? I don't understand.' I leaned forward onto my elbows, trying for a bit of intimidation. 'He knows it now, four days later.'

'That's very nice,' she repeated. 'I'm glad. He'll almost certainly do better on the next test.'

'How about a retest? Just to see what he knows,' I suggested.

'Absolutely not,' she said. 'I'm sorry, Mr. Edwards, but my policy does not allow for retesting. I expect students to keep up. It isn't fair to my other students if I offer Danny a retest.'

'Why?' I asked, genuinely wanting an answer. 'What does it have to do with them? Isn't the test about what he knows or doesn't know?'

'By the deadline, yes.'

'By the deadline? It was only four days ago. What if he'd been absent? I didn't keep him home; I guess I should have.'

'He would have taken the test on Wednesday when he had my class again.'

'You're . . . you're kidding,' I let go with a frustrated sigh, couldn't have kept it in with a gun to my head. 'I made him come to school so you could punish him.'

'I don't make him play soccer, Mr. Edwards.'

'Well, suppose that he –'

'Students have to learn to respect deadlines,' she interrupted again, the hairy farm animal.

'Sure,' I agreed, 'to respect them.'

'What happens at work if you ignore deadlines?' She opted to answer her own question. 'You get fired.'

'No I don't,' I said, struggling to keep it polite. I'd promised Danny I wouldn't shout or use bad language or threaten to cook and eat one of Mrs. Werner's twenty-three cats. 'I don't get fired, and if that's what teachers are telling students today, you should stop.' She didn't respond right away, so I went on. 'If I miss a deadline, I stay late, get up early, convince my boss that

I'll make it priority, and I get it done . . . which is exactly what my son is trying to do right now.'

She shook her head; every stiff hair moved collaboratively like quills on a porcupine. She stared down at the connect-the-dots map of liver spots on her hands. 'All right. If you're interested in knowing how he might fare on the test and how he's done reviewing this week, I'll have him take it Monday.'

'And give him the better grade?'

'I'll average the two of them together,' she said and rose from the chair. 'That's the best I can offer, if you're convinced he's done the work.'

I should've kept my mouth shut. I didn't and regretted the next thirty seconds all afternoon. 'How does that make any sense at all?'

Startled, Mrs. Werner looked as if she might withdraw her offer and then invade France . . . by herself. She stared at me in stupid silence. Clearly, there weren't many people around Robert Morris High School willing to call Alfrieda Werner an idiot, at least not to her face.

I said, 'Really . . . if he knows the math today, why average his grade with a test he took on a day when we all agree he didn't know what he was doing? How can that make any sense?'

Again, she didn't answer. Rather, she said simply, 'I'll see him Monday morning at seven. Have him review Chapter Nine this weekend.' She turned to go.

'Mrs. Werner?' Having insulted her, I tried to iron out a few wrinkles before she escaped, and hoped she wouldn't take *my* bad behavior out on my son.

'Yes, Mr. Edwards?' Irritated, she turned on me, quick for her age.

'Do you have a business card, ma'am?'

'A business card?' She hadn't expected that.

'Yes, ma'am,' I said. 'Can I have one, you know, with your phone number and email?'

She drew a neatly printed card from a sweater pocket. It sported the school's crest and motto in a tidy, polite font. Brandishing a condescending grin, she asked, 'May I have one of yours as well?'

'Sure,' I added my home phone and personal email on the back. 'Call any time.'

For about two decades, I had carried a collection of business cards in my wallet. Not my own cards, I needed only a few of those each year. Rather, I carried a dozen or so cards I scavenged from people I genuinely disliked, even a couple I despised, my ex-wife's attorney, for example.

There was one from the wine steward at the local shop, another snide prick who never missed an opportunity to make me feel stupid about my choice of wine based on rainfall totals in the Médoc as opposed to the Loire regions. What kind of frigging sex life does a person like that have?

I had one from the group insurance sales representative who visited my office twice each year to convince me that if I were to fall over dead, my children would be destitute within an hour.

I'd stolen two from the knuckle-dragging simian who always managed to find $1,400 of necessary repairs to my car, no matter why I'd brought it into the shop. I swear I could drive to the garage for a $29.99 oil change and arrive home that afternoon having run up $900 on my VISA with no noticeable difference in how the car ran.

Next in the stack was my neighbor, the one who allows his dogs to use my backyard as an outhouse and never picks up after them. I had three of his cards for special occasions. It was a wonder he never asked why I so frequently requested another, the jackass. He's such an egomaniacal lardass he probably thought I was just *that* impressed with his title, Store Manager.

Yeah, that gets me all aflutter.

I never sat alone flipping through business cards of people I hated, fawning over them like some sociopath with a rambling manifesto beneath my mattress. Rather, I used them in what I thought was a deft transfer of my animosity for one person to another I also disliked. Here's how it worked: If in the course of my day, I encountered a true moron – everyone knows them, can see them coming, people who clearly need to be shipped off to the deep end of someplace disagreeable; the North Sea works – but if I happened to be unfortunate enough to encounter one of these roving monkey farts, I would find a way to pass along my honest sentiment, generally scrawled in nasty terms on the back of a business card from my collection.

For example, if a pushy, suburbanite, PTA mom elbows past me in line just to dump twenty-two items on the fifteen-item conveyor, especially if I only have one or two things in my basket, I might leave an insulting note on her windshield: *IS THAT YOUR ASS, OR ARE YOU STORING CHRISTMAS ROASTS BACK THERE?*

Granted, not my best effort, but it works as an example.

I don't deliver these messages on my own business cards, however. Instead, I carefully write my *CHRISTMAS ROAST* insult on someone else's card, my auto mechanic or my loser neighbor for instance, and then enjoy the afternoon knowing I've packaged my dislike for one person and passed it on to someone else, someone disdainful.

Do they ever contact one another and begin shouting? Punching? Throwing rocks?

Who cares? For me, it's enough just to take my animosity for one shitbag and hand it off to another shitbag, as cathartic as decaf tea and a hot bath.

That Friday, as I left Morris High School, I decided to stop for coffee. Already ten dollars light in my coffee budget with no useful results, I turned toward Dunkin' Donuts, thinking I might also indulge in a Bavarian cream in hopes of purging old Werner's acrid taste from my throat. Crossing Center Street with a green light, I stood on my brakes when some lunatic in a behemoth, crimson Ford SVT, the one with the twenty-seven-cylinder engine, pulled in front of me with a throaty roar through a glass-pack exhaust pipe. My tires wailed discontent; my car fishtailed, the ass end swerving dangerously into oncoming traffic before overcorrecting right and slapping against the curb with a tooth-rattling thunk that sent my rear hubcap rolling into a drainage ditch full of soupy mud and old Taco Bell wrappers.

'Sonofabitch!' I shouted, hoping the Cro-Magnon driving spoke American profanity. 'Limp dick sonofawhore! Watch where you're going, you ape!'

Already nearly a block away, the crimson giant ignored me, but turned without signaling onto Benson Avenue into the Dunkin' Donuts lot.

Now I stood on the gas. My car, an old Taurus, could barely get out of its own way and only growled an asthmatic response. But I hustled toward the donut shop, hoping to run the ugly bastard over then bask in the mundane pleasure of a Bavarian cream while his blood dried in a tacky smear on my shattered grille.

Muttering threats, I squealed into the lot, pulled up behind the Ford and skidded to a stop.

He wasn't there.

I got out. My door propped open, my car still running, I turned to the glass front of the donut shop, thinking I'd spot him inside, perhaps punch his lights out.

Nothing.

Then I realized: Route 9's Dunkin' Donuts shares the corner of 9 and Benson with a Gold's Gym, the weight lifting place where steroid babies go to pump themselves up in the mirror. Like my just-below-average performance in high school math, my weight lifting acumen ranked somewhere south of middle-aged man but north of chubby fourth grader. Needless to say, I'd not spent much time pumping iron at Gold's, but the man – the glandular anomaly – entering the gym's wide double doors right now, almost as broad across as he was tall, clearly did.

Lifting weights at 10:00 on a Friday morning . . . if I'd ever wondered who could possibly lift weights at 10:00 on a Friday morning, I now had my answer: a Cro-Magnon, steroid baby, two-hundred-eighty pounds of Clydesdale muscle, bad attitude, and double . . . check that . . . *triple*-parked Ford SVT Raptor, blood-red pickup truck.

That's who.

All the fight left me.

This man would break me into pieces, write greeting cards with his 64-pack of Crayola crayons, and send my best bits off to his relatives in

Lapland where I'd be barbecued and eaten before the interior lights in my Taurus even dimmed. Challenging him physically was immediately out of the question.

I opted for donuts instead, always preferable to violent confrontation. I figured if I took my time we'd all die of Type-II Diabetes.

Ten minutes later, I left Dunkin' Donuts, coffee in hand, Bavarian cream in my sated belly, and diabolical thoughts of vengeance alive in my imagination.

Old Mrs. Werner's business card all but burned a hole in my shirt pocket.

Somewhere across the street, Cro-Magnon lifted 400 pounds over his head, put it down, picked it up, put it down, picked it up . . . yeah, like that.

And somewhere up Route 9, Alfrieda Werner tortured innocent students with incoherent references to trigonometric functions, while Richard Wagner's *Die Walküre* provided scratchy background music on a classroom record player, just for dramatic celebration of *Der Vaterland*.

These two needed to meet.

Heh.

Balancing the coffee on the hood of my car, I dug in my briefcase for a pen, then scribbled a brief message on Mrs. Werner's business card: *NICE PARKING JOB, DOUCHE BAG. YOUR MOM TEACH YOU THAT?*

I thought twice, even three times about using "douche bag" and wondered if I might smudge the letters somewhat and change it to read *LIMP TWAT*. I'd never liked "douche bag" as an insult and regretted writing it. However, I decided to leave it alone for a couple of reasons.

First, I was sure beyond any doubt that Mrs. Werner often went home, fired up a double helping of *spätzle*, and referred to students, my son included, as "douche bags."

Jesus, I hated that woman.

Second, as much as I wanted to use the word "twat" for its versatility and generalizability, I doubted that Cro-Magnon knew entirely what a twat was.

So I went with *DOUCHE BAG*, much to my own shame and embarrassment.

With a sip of coffee, I finished the message, affixed Werner's card to the Ford's windshield, just by the corner; so it would stick up far enough for him to see it, and then – encouraged that I'd avoided two opportunities for *episodic rage* – drove to work, wondering how anyone lifting weights at 10:00 on a Friday morning could afford a $60,000 truck.

The day passed in relative calm. I spent the weekend watching Danny play soccer in a south Jersey tournament and didn't give another thought to Cro-Magnon or Alfrieda Werner.

That proved to be a mistake.

On Monday afternoon, Danny showed up early from school; soccer practice had been canceled.

Wordlessly, he handed me a wrinkled piece of letterhead with an official statement from Principal Kieffer.

'What's up?' I asked, glancing at the few cramped paragraphs. 'Tuberculosis outbreak? Lennie kill a rabbit?'

He shook his head, didn't look well.

'Danny?'

'Dad, Mrs. Werner's dead.'

'Dead?' Now I read the letter, alternately looking down at the text and over at my son. 'What? How? What happened?'

'Somebody killed her.' He slumped on the sofa, looked drawn, deflated. 'No one knows, but the rumors are bad. Jackson told Casey that he'd heard one of the guidance counselors tell the library assistant lady that she'd been beaten with a hammer.'

'Jesus Christ!' I let the principal's note drop and crossed to sit beside him. 'C'mon, Danny, no way. I mean . . . where would she go? She wasn't leaving work for anyplace dangerous. How could that have happened?'

He shrugged. 'Someone broke into her house, I guess.'

The tumblers keeping my memories safely in check clicked into place. I replayed my meeting with her Friday morning, her business card, and the Cro-Magnon's frightening pickup, sanguine and triple parked, daring anyone to challenge him.

My mind raced full throttle through the hour after leaving Morris High with Mrs. Werner's business card and my arrival at work, Dunkin' Donuts cup in hand:

Did I leave fingerprints?

Of course you did.

Can they match the handwriting to mine?

Of course they can. You didn't do anything to disguise it, shithead.

But that doesn't matter. I didn't kill her.

But you pushed the snowball down the hill, and she's still dead.

Does anyone know I argued with her in the conference room?

Only people she told at school. Okay, and people you told at work.

'Dad?'

But it doesn't matter. I didn't kill her.

It does matter. She's dead. And the police are going to have questions.

Jesus . . . Jesus Christ, she had a copy of my business card in that ghastly sweater. With your handwriting.

'Dad!'

And my fingerprints.

How easy will those be to match with the card on the truck?

Pretty easy.

But if they never find the card from the truck . . . if the guy gets away with it.
Jesus Jumping Christ, listen to yourself!

'Dad!' Danny shouted.

'What? What is it?'

'It's on the news.' He flipped to channel 12. 'Watch.'

We listened as neatly-quaffed Barbie and Ken dolls described, in tastefully grim terms, Mrs. Alfrieda Werner's grisly death at the hands of an assailant who, police believe, broke into her home in search of prescription drugs or valuables.

Danny groaned softly when Ken noted that, 'Werner, a long-time math teacher at Robert Morris High School had been beaten with a blunt instrument, perhaps a hammer.'

'Holy shit,' I whispered. 'This isn't good.'

Danny shushed me to listen as Barbie wrapped up. '. . . students and teachers are in shock tonight. Principal Kieffer plans to release viewing and funeral arrangements to the community in the next few days. Interested parents will find additional information on the school's web site.'

'Horrible news from out there at Morris High,' Ken shuffled papers, looked over at Barbie for confirmation that he'd employed just the right touch of pathos.

'Terrible news, just terrible,' Barbie echoed, adding a pained grimace for good measure. To the camera, she said, 'We'll be back in a moment with your five-day forecast.'

Danny clicked off the television. 'Who could do something like that? I mean, beat an old lady.'

I know exactly who, Danny, and he's a monster, as big as a porta-john, probably lost in a demented steroid rage right now, trying to scrub blood out of his floor mats.

'I dunno, buddy,' I said. 'There are dangerous people out there, willing to do just about anything to get money for drugs.'

'But they're not sure that was the reason. Right? I mean, they didn't say anything about drugs or money being missing.'

'That's true,' I didn't like seeing him this frightened, tried some levity. 'Maybe it was a former student, you know, someone who ended the year with a D+, maybe thought he deserved a C-.'

His face lit with a lovely amalgam of guilt and conspiratorial humor. 'Dad!' He slugged me in the shoulder. 'That's terrible!'

'Yeah,' I laughed, couldn't help it, 'I know, but keep in mind, if she'd maybe throttle back on the homework, people around here wouldn't –'

My doorbell rang.

For the next two hours, I worked like a savant to keep lies and omissions straight in my head, and this despite the ever burgeoning hole in the pit of my stomach, if there is such a thing.

Detective Janet Siegrist spent the vestiges of the afternoon at my dining table, alternately looking as if she might put me in handcuffs or sneak a quick nap. An exhausted, big-boned, middle-aged woman, not unattractive but not at all sexy, she drank black coffee like an intergalactic champion as she rolled back and forth over the same set of repetitive questions.

'And the nature of your conversation with Mrs. Werner Friday morning?'

'I had concerns about my son's grade on a recent test.'

'You say you were with her for . . .' she trailed off, leading me by an investigative leash.

'Twenty minutes, give or take.'

'And you gave her a business card because she asked for one?'

'She did.'

'Why's that?'

'Why not? To contact me, if necessary, regarding Danny's progress the rest of this semester.'

And in as casual a tone as if she might ask for more sugar, Detective Siegrist said, 'Did you ask for one of hers?'

Just to throw her off, I asked, 'One of her what?'

'A business card, Mr. Edwards,' she lifted hangdog eyes from a spiral notebook. Siegrist apparently hadn't graduated to the iPad chapter in the *Interrogation Manual* yet. 'Did you ask for one of her business cards?'

'Um . . . no,' I tried to sound convincing.

'Why's that?'

Make eye contact. Throw casual right back at her.

'I dunno,' I said. 'I guess because all of her contact information is on her syllabus, or because I can always just call the school. I have that number memorized; it's easier than, you know, digging for a card all the time.'

Okay, that's a lie.

'So . . . you don't have a copy of Mrs. Werner's business card?'

'Nope,' I shrugged, then asked, 'Is this relevant, somehow, to catching the killer? Did he leave her business card somewhere? Is there some connection?'

Siegrist ignored me. Slugging more coffee, she returned to her questions. 'All right, Mr. Edwards, one more time, and I'm sure we're done.'

'Go right ahead,' I said, fussing over a paper napkin Danny had left on the table.

'You went to the school at around . . .'

And we worked through Detective Siegrist's prompts again.

Fifteen minutes later, she rose to leave. I noticed a modest, gold pendant around her neck, *27*, and considered asking what it meant. So oddly incongruous with the rest of her no-nonsense, Wal-Mart appearance, the one bit of deliberate frill and beauty must have been important. But I decided not to, didn't want her to misunderstand any compliment or think I was trying to Vegas my way out of trouble.

Instead, I shook her hand and promised to call if I thought of anything that might assist her investigation. Before she left, however, I did ask, have no idea why, 'Detective, do you have a card? You know . . . with your contact information?'

When Siegrist glanced over this time, her rheumy look of distracted fatigue faded, and a determined blood hound stared back at me. The fleck of amiable *27* disappeared inside her wash-and-wear blouse.

Siegrist handed me a card. 'Sure thing,' and I should have felt it coming, should have known she would want to watch my face, see me react to her request. 'Can I have one of yours, sir?'

Panic flooded my bloodstream, freezing me to the spot for just a second too long. With pinpricks of cool sweat forming above my hairline – she could smell me perspiring; I swear to God her nostrils flared – I finally slapped myself lucid and tugged my wallet from my khakis. 'Here you are, Detective. Call me anytime.'

Turning to go, she glanced back long enough to add, 'You know, I had her about a hundred years ago, when she was still over at Jefferson. She failed me fall semester, senior year, Advanced Math. I had to make it up in night school.'

I didn't know what to say. 'Really? So . . . you know her. Knew her?'

'Yeah,' Siegrist nodded. 'She was a bitch, even back then when she was young . . . younger, whatever.'

I shrugged, didn't want to commit either way on the 'bitch' comment. 'Good night, Detective. I'll call if I think of anything.'

I met Siegrist again about a week later, when she invited Danny and me to the police station in Freehold. When I asked why Danny had to come, she insisted that it was just a formality in case they had questions for him regarding his transformations of functions test and studying for the retake. My alibi for the murder weekend was oak strong; I'd been at Danny's tournament in Atlantic County. Dozens of people had seen me. I'd eaten dinner with the team on Friday and Saturday, had driven two of Danny's teammates back to the hotel both nights, and had been with my son after they'd been eliminated from the semi-final game around 3:00 Sunday afternoon.

There was no possible way I could have been the one to bludgeon Mrs. Werner to death . . . as much as I might've wanted to.

No way.

At the station, a kid young enough to look like he was playing dress-up in a police uniform escorted me to Siegrist's office. In jeans and an exhausted wool blazer, she rose to greet me, her inexpensive tastes hanging from her broad frame like so much laundry. I wondered what she enjoyed watching on Sunday afternoons when she did all her own ironing. Apparently, cops didn't make enough to afford regular dry cleaning.

She asked the same set of questions she'd brought to my house. I remembered my lie, about Werner's business card, and stuck to it, answering as causally and off-handedly as I could feign, but nailing the response almost perfectly: with just enough uncertainty overlain with tepid confidence.

'Yes, sure . . . that's right. No, I'm positive, Detective; I didn't ask her for a card. Nope. I didn't.'

Yeah. Not bad.

When she requested a writing sample, I panicked a bit. Siegrist knew I would; it's probably why she'd brought me to the station, to watch me squirm on the hook when she asked for something I hadn't anticipated.

'Why?' I said. 'Why would you need a writing sample?'

'Again, Mr. Edwards, you don't have to; it's just a formality.'

Now you're lying, bonehead. I could stall this whole process, insist on being read my rights, hire an attorney, clam up, or just leave. I could do all of that . . . but I won't. Because I didn't kill her.

I played scared for a minute. 'Um . . . do I need a lawyer?'

'You're not under arrest. I'm just asking you to cooperate with the investigation, help us out a little. I'll admit that we have few leads in this case; the trail's getting cold on this one, and I'm trying to be thorough.'

Tell her. Jesus, tell her who did it. Tell her you know it was that frigging Cro-Magnon from Gold's Gym, the big guy with the red pickup.

I can't say why, but I decided to meet Detective Siegrist half way. I wouldn't pass along what I knew about the red pickup, about the man I suspected murdered Mrs. Werner. He must've left some evidence behind, some trail or clues. These Bozos just couldn't figure it out. Maybe an anonymous tip would work. It worked in dime novels and bad movies. Perhaps I could find a way to send an anonymous tip with a description of the killer, the suspect, the linebacker in the red truck, whatever he was.

That decision made me feel better, and I acquiesced on the handwriting sample. 'Sure, Detective,' I even smiled. 'What can I write for you?'

She passed me a legal-looking document with my name, the date, her name and contact information listed in various blanks and fields across the top. Siegrist pointed to a rectangular box dominating the lower half of the sheet. 'In here, Mr. Edwards, would you please write the alphabet, the numbers from one to ten, and the following list of words.'

She handed me a 3 x 5 index card on which someone had printed, in capital letters, a column of stand-alone words:

NICE

YOUR
PARKING
MOM
JOB
TEACH
THAT
DOUCHE BAG

Seeing the words, *DOUCHE BAG*, I stopped. 'Detective, I don't really like this insult . . . here at the bottom. Do you need me to . . .'

She nodded, knowing she had me. 'Yessir, sorry about that, but I do need you to write all of the words in the column.' Her gold *27* pendant glinted. 'Please.'

I held my breath for about ten seconds, hoped she didn't notice. Instead of my usual, blocky, all-caps printing, I reverted to a cursive style I'd perfected thirty-five years earlier in Monmouth County's public school system. Third grade, Mrs. Helms. I'd used it all through college, had friends who teased me about how neatly I wrote, scripted love letters to my ex-wife, homework assignments, even half-drunk notes on dorm room doors at 3:00 a.m. Like shooting a free throw or parallel parking, the cursive muscle memory came back without a hitch. I wrote Siegrist's quickie assessment with distracted confidence.

Only after I finished the last words, *DOUCHE BAG*, did I panic again.

Swallowing, the dry walls of my throat clamped together; I avoided eye contact, certain Siegrist would read blatant guilt in my face.

Staring at the page, I waited for her to read me my rights, to search her desk for a pair of handcuffs, to explain to Danny that he'd have to call his mother because Dear Old Dad would be her guest for the night in the county lockup.

None of that happened.

In five minutes, I was reunited with Danny in the lobby. Detective Carlisle, a young guy, obviously mentoring under Siegrist, walked us out, chatting until we reached my car. He'd played soccer in high school and was interested in the ins and outs of our college search. Teasing Danny, he asked, 'So how far can you kick a ball on the fly? Unimpeded, unchallenged, you know what I mean. How far? Fifty yards?'

Danny beamed, 'Seventy three!'

I jumped in. 'Um . . . seventy *two* at his last assessment.'

Carlisle shot us both an incredulous look. 'Seventy-two yards? Holy crap.'

'Yeah,' Danny said. 'We have a guy on the team who can basically kick the length of the field. He's looking at Stanford.'

'Meh, you'll get there,' Carlisle offered a playful shove, then opened

Danny's door, 'just as soon as you grow into those feet. Good grief, what size are those?'

'Thirteens!'

'Just like his Dad,' I waggled a loafer for his inspection. 'Like father like son.'

Danny talked all the way home about how Detective Carlisle bought him a Coke and asked about Manalapan Galaxy soccer tournaments, even the games that weekend when they'd lost in the semifinals on Sunday.

Checking my alibi again, Siegrist? Good dog.

It was nearly a month later, our lives having returned to normal, as normal as lives get for single parents with busy teenagers, when the first card appeared on my windshield.

I pushed a shopping cart through the grocery store parking lot, loaded bags into my back seat, then dutifully shoved the cart toward the corral. I flipped through texts on my phone, slid into the driver's seat, and inserted the key before noticing the card there, print side down, beneath my windshield wiper.

ROBERT MORRIS HIGH SCHOOL
ALFRIEDA WERNER
Mathematics Instructor/Department Chair

Mrs. Werner's email and phone number were too small to decipher without my glasses, but I could easily make out the school's motto. Danny carried a notebook with a worn sticker affixed off center to its cover: *LEARN, ACHIEVE, CREATE.*

'What the hell?' I sat dumbstruck a moment. 'No, this isn't . . .' Stupidly, I checked my phone as if a rational answer might appear on the screen. 'Hey . . . wait . . . just wait.'

Retrieving the card with uncertain fingers, I didn't need glasses to read the note scribbled in limp cursive on the opposite side: *NICE PARKING JOB, DOUCHE BAG. YOUR MOM TEACH YOU THAT?*

I turned a slow, deliberate circle, scanning the lot while breathing slowly, in my nose and out my mouth. I'd read an article in *People* a few years back suggesting it was an effective means of calming down in stressful situations.

Probably baloney.

My mind pinged from impossible to improbable to unreasonable as I considered a salad bar of incongruous means by which bludgeoned and dead Alfrieda Werner's business card ended up on my windshield six weeks after her murder.

And I saw him, the red pickup, a frigging automotive monolith, parked like a slumbering beast in an alley behind a hardware store. From this far away I couldn't hear the engine rumble like a dragon's purr, but I imagined it terrifying enough.

A warm splash of urine wet my boxers, spotted my khakis with an embarrassing stain. I didn't care.

He knew. He knew, and he watched me – wanting to see what I'd do, how I'd react when I understood that I was utterly screwed.

So with a burgeoning Rorschach blot darkening my crotch, I stared into the truck's tinted window, tore the business card with deliberate defiance, and dropped the shreds to the pavement.

It didn't matter, didn't scare him off.

Redolent of piss and useless defiance, I drove home.

More cards followed.

Three days later, outside my office, in a city lot that saw hundreds of people pass through each day:

ROBERT MORRIS HIGH SCHOOL
ALFRIEDA WERNER
Mathematics Instructor/Department Chair
NICE PARKING JOB . . .

I dropped my briefcase and ran, didn't quite know where I was going. But I needed to catch him, wanted to locate his truck, to confront him in broad daylight with witnesses poised to dial 911 when he began tearing my throat out. I jogged a lap of the lot, not finding the crimson beast, but imagining that throaty growl down every side street, pulling away from every intersection, the same insidious roar I remembered from outside my favorite Dunkin' Donuts.

. . . YOUR MOM TEACH YOU THAT?

How to cower like a terrified fourth grader? With wet pants, sucking my thumb, and wishing I could turn back time?

No. My mom didn't teach me that.

Familiar rage, mercurial and blinding, tried to conquer me right there. I fought it, sat in the cold grass, counting breaths until it subsided. Attacking this man would do me no good; it would only get me badly beaten or worse. I'd have to deal with him another way.

A week later, Sunday, outside a movie theater where I'd taken Danny:

ROBERT MORRIS HIGH SCHOOL
ALFRIEDA WERNER
Mathematics Instructor/Department Chair
. . . YOUR MOM TEACH YOU THAT? in loopy script.

This time I didn't piss myself, didn't take off running, didn't yell or curse or shake my fist at traffic on Route 9. Instead, I palmed the card and calmly clicked the automatic locks for Danny.

'What's that?' He asked, not caring much.

'Nothing,' I coughed over the tremor in my voice, 'some Chinese place over on 33, must've just opened.'

'We should go,' he dropped inside the car. 'We never go for Chinese.'

'Yeah, we can go if you're hungry.'

'And just think,' he leaned over so I'd hear him, 'in a week, I can drive you for Chinese.'

'Sure, sure. Another week. But first you gotta show me that you can parallel park.'

'Aunt Heather can't parallel park, and she's almost forty five.'

'Good point,' I admitted. 'However, she has a Master's degree. Get one of those and you don't have to parallel park. It's New Jersey law; trust me.'

'Hey,' he changed the subject. 'Have you seen my running watch? I can't find it.'

'Have you checked the floor of that demilitarized disaster you call a room?'

'Um . . . no.'

'I suggest you start there.'

'I wanna run some intervals tomorrow and need to time myself.' He extended a naked wrist in my direction as if I might conjure up a watch through sheer force of will. 'Do you still have yours?'

'Somewhere. You can borrow it.'

It passed, that quickly. I didn't confess, didn't warn him, didn't suggest that perhaps he should watch for a Dracula-red Raptor with tinted windows and big-dick tires, didn't tell him that he might come home one afternoon to find his father beaten to bloody soup by the same man-creature who killed his Algebra teacher. Nope. None of that. Instead, I took a quick glance around, caught sight of a shadowy Ford idling outside a 7-Eleven, dropped the card, piled into my car with a half box of Milk Duds in my jacket, and drove my son to a Chinese restaurant for Szechuan chicken.

Cro-Magnon left me alone for over a week. I thought we might be through, that he might have decided I'd gone to the police. I mean, I had evidence that he stole business cards from Werner's house, at least two of them. Well, I *had* evidence; I didn't any longer. In my panic and haste, I'd destroyed both cards, stupid. I should have taken them to Siegrist right away. Granted, I'd have to admit that I'd been lying about the original card, but she might forgive that transgression when I handed over a substantial connection between Cro-Magnon and the victim. Alfrieda Werner sure as hell wasn't driving around town handing out her own cards.

I vowed I'd take the very next one to the police.

I didn't.

But it wasn't my fault.

Late that week, Danny and I picked up groceries together. I carried two bags, so he jogged ahead to open the car. 'I'm driving!'

'Fine,' I called after, 'you're driving. Why don't you impress me by opening the door so I can put these bags –'

I watched it happen. The whole works – noticing, reaching, tugging, reading – might've taken two seconds. But in my stunned silence, it seemed like all afternoon. I called again, trying anything. 'No, Danny, wait! Hey!'

Surprised, he turned, the card pinched nonchalantly between two fingers. 'Jesus, Dad, what's wrong? You all right?'

'Yeah, yeah,' my mind tore headlong through a list of idiotic possibilities. 'It's just these bags . . . they're really tearing into my fingers.' I offered him both. 'Here.'

He reached for one, kept Werner's business card in his opposite hand; it might as well have been ten miles away. I couldn't get to it without tackling him.

Shit and shit and shit.

'Here,' he took a plastic bag, tossed it on the back seat. 'C'mon, that thing can't be more than five pounds. You all right?'

'Yeah,' I reached for the card, tried to take it from him without appearing desperate. 'Yeah, I . . . you know . . . I got a paper cut on my finger this morning. That bag was just pressing right on it.'

'Sure, that's like NAZI torture, no doubt.'

'Hey, wiseass,' I missed – *goddamnit* – dropped the other bag on the back seat, closed the door, and sweating, turned to find him reading.

'Nice parking job, douche bag . . . oh, Dad, you hate that. Look, some jackass put this on the car.' He went on, 'Your mom teach you that?' He laughed. 'Heh. Your mom teach you that? Nice people in this town. Huh? I mean, you're not the greatest at parking, but this isn't bad. And nice handwriting, too, cursive, like you and Mom taught me.' He waved the card, more amused than frightened or offended. I figured it had something to do with social media; in my day getting a hand-written insult on your windshield would have been a shocker. Today, maybe not.

'Lemme see that.' Again, I reached, looking like an idiot.

'See?' He read again, 'Nice parking job . . .'

And God or the Universe or some benevolent force decided in that moment to look down on me and smile. I hadn't been catching many breaks that month, but in the two seconds that it took my son to come up with an insult for his wimpy, paper-cut father, I was able to assert a thimble of authority and take the card from him. He never turned it over; thank Christ.

I did.

ROBERT MORRIS HIGH SCHOOL
ALFRIEDA WERNER
Mathematics Instructor/Department Chair
And in the distance, that same guttural warning rumbled an octave

lower than ambient traffic. I didn't even bother looking around. I had Siegrist's card in my wallet; I could call her right now, confess everything to Danny, admit that I'd been involved in Mrs. Werner's death, albeit tangentially. We needed to make the right decision, needed to –

He snatched the card from me, quick as a boardwalk magician. 'I'll take care of it.' He tore it up, dramatically ripping halves into quarters, then eighths. When he couldn't pull off sixteenths, Danny grimaced and tossed the makeshift confetti over his head. 'There, that does it.'

A quick attack of vertigo threatened to drop me on my ass. 'Yeah, heh,' I managed. 'That'll show him. Now, let's get out of here before the county police pick you up for littering.'

'I'm driving!'

'No,' I started.

'Why not? I gotta practice before my test.'

Why not? Well, Danny, because I prefer to be behind the wheel in case that prehistoric monster decides to crush us like a Pepsi can.

He tried again. 'Dad?'

'Yeah, sorry,' I said finally. 'You drive. Who knows what I might do with this paper cut? Maybe crash us into a ditch.'

The following day I called in sick – flu, whatever – and spent the morning at Dunkin' Donuts. I waited, watching the parking lot and trying to decide what I might do if Cro-Magnon showed up.

He didn't.

So I called in sick again, *nasty bug; yeah, thanks . . . I'm sure I'll shake it soon.*

And waited again.

It was almost 10:30, when he finally arrived, rolling into the shared lot, a bloody sea beast breaching across two parking spaces and crowding a miniature Kia Soul into a grimy spot beside an aromatic dumpster.

He got out, all three-hundred-whatever pounds of him, stringy black hair falling over his shoulders, his calves, in cutoff sweatpants, looking like dinner plates.

I couldn't image what he did for a living. Anything other than *cook and distribute crystal methamphetamine to middle schoolers* would have rung as too improbable to believe.

He didn't look my way, didn't see my car – I'd parked on the other side of the building. He just shouldered his gym bag and half stalked, half glided into the gym, ready once again to inject himself with human growth hormone before pumping iron, more weight in two hours than I'd lifted in my entire life. Not kidding.

I forced myself to wait another twenty minutes, actually counted down from 180 for the last three as my hands shook and sweat beaded between my shoulder blades.

I had no idea what I planned to do. I wasn't armed, hadn't prepared a threatening speech, didn't even have Detective Siegrist's phone number handy.

Still questioning my behavior, I mined in my wallet for a business card – not one of my own. Rather, I located an old one, the handyman who screwed me on a bathroom job a few years back, then screwed my wife for a month afterward. He'd over charged me then dragged his feet when the toilet leaked. I eventually spent six months filing insurance paperwork to replace $2750 in flooring and downstairs sheetrock, none of which Handy Joe covered.

Well, Joe . . . let's see how handy you are if King Kong decides to pay you a visit.

My fingers still shaking, I wrote – in my same, college script:
LEAVE ME AND MY FAMILY ALONE, OR I'LL TELL THE POLICE WHAT YOU DID.

It wasn't tough, wasn't going to win me any Clint Eastwood Badass Award for clenched-teeth determination. But it got the point across: I had one recourse against this man, calling Siegrist. If he knew it, maybe he'd put two and two together and realize that I was the only variable keeping him out of prison.

I slipped the card beneath his windshield wiper, made a miraculous recovery from the flu, and hit my office for a few hours. My boss, concerned for my welfare, chased me out after lunch. Thanking her, I left around 2:00, stopped at Target for a few items, and held my breath when I approached the car, trying to make out my windshield from ten spaces away.

Nothing.

There. See? It's done. Nice work. Reason and logic prevail once again.

With groceries on the passenger seat, I drove home, trying hard not to think about the fact that I was the only variable keeping Cro-Magnon out of prison. While I saw that as productive, he might see it differently.

At home, I felt good. Flipping on some music, I sang along with Taylor Grande Ariana Swift as I brewed coffee and thought about watching a movie or reading until Danny came home hungry from soccer practice. He'd passed his driving test and was running himself back and forth to school this week, a welcome change for him, another reason to worry for me.

Instead, I decided to be useful and went upstairs to gather some laundry. I grabbed the hamper from my closet, the towels from my bathroom, and dredged up the array of clean, dirty, condemned, infected, and gruesome articles from Danny's bedroom floor. Tossing it all in the hamper, I started downstairs then stopped by his bathroom, figuring I'd wash his towels, too.

'Might need a second load,' I sang tunelessly to myself. 'I'm just-a, just-a, just-a, just-a doing laundry all day, a just-a washing towels and filthy soccer shorts and –'

The song died in my throat.

Instead, I let go with a wheeze, air through a dog's broken chew toy. I dropped the hamper, didn't feel or even hear it land at my feet. Covering my mouth and nose with both hands, I leaned in to the mirror, my son's bathroom mirror, above the mess of shaving cream, deodorant, toothbrushes, slimy soap, and acne medication.

Taped to the mirror, crookedly, off center, was Alfrieda Werner's business card with one word in block letters: *NO.*

Jesus. Jesus, help me. Jesus, he was in my house, in my house, in my son's bathroom. In my house.

Toppling forward, I almost fell, then caught myself against Danny's sink. I stared down at a glob of dry toothpaste clinging to the slippery bowl, took in its texture, the irregular shape. Some part of me hoped that if I looked away long enough the card would disappear.

It didn't. Still clinging stubbornly with a ragged square of scotch tape, it teased me, dared me to do anything at all.

Go to the police?

He'll know. He'll kill Danny and you before they get anywhere near him.

Threaten him?

Tried that already.

Kill him?

Sure. Right. Yeah, just commit murder; add that to your to-do list this week.

The few reasonable brain cells left unsupervised in my mind pulled together in the interests of communicating one clear message: *Danny!*

'No, no!' I bounded downstairs, found my wallet, phone, and keys, made sure to lock the front door, and was in my car in less than twenty seconds. At 2:45 p.m. on a weekday, Danny was still at soccer practice behind the high school. I covered the three miles in record time, checking side streets, driveways, parking lots, even shadowy places beneath trees along the way in hopes of spotting the blood-thirsty Ford with its grinning grill of sharpened teeth.

It wasn't on the road between my house and the school; it wasn't in the parking lot, and it wasn't behind the building near the playing fields. I found Danny's car in the student section, drove slowly past, and checked his windshield. There were no cards, no evidence that anyone had been here to threaten him or leave messages for me.

I turned off the engine, sat in blissful silence for several minutes, then reached for my phone.

I had to confess.

Mrs. Werner rose up in my imagination. Her skull cracked open, her hair matted with dry blood and gory bits of something unfathomable. She offered investigating officers a yellow-toothed grimace, a look of permanent shock and disdain, forever communicating her animosity, despite the fact that her head resembled a partially deflated basketball dipped in nightmarish automobile wreckage.

Behind her corpse stood a neatly organized desk, Teutonic, everything in its place: two gold pens, a dictionary, a framed photo of an athletic young man, monogrammed envelopes and stationery, a half empty mug of English breakfast tea, an Agatha Christie mystery on loan from the library, and a stack of business cards. He'd beaten her to death, left her scalp in puckered, tattered rags, then stopped – blood splattered and smelling of fresh corpse and elderly woman piss, no-nonsense soap – long enough to think about me.

He thought about me then stole a stack of business cards, just slipped them inside his flannel shirt, reminding himself to take them out before rinsing her blood from his clothes.

Detective Siegrist expressed only mild surprise hearing from me. 'Come in, Mr. Edwards. It's nice to see you again.'

I hesitated in the door frame, waiting in case she decided to read me my Miranda rights. Rather, she stood beside her desk and gestured to an uncomfortable looking wooden chair.

'Coffee?'

'Um . . . yeah, thanks.' I waited while she dialed up two black coffees from someone down the hall.

She hung up, leaned forward, elbows on her desk. 'So . . . what should we talk about?'

'You know?' I read her face. 'You know!'

'Know what? Do I know that you have information you believe is important to our investigation? I've suspected that. Yes. Do I know what you've been doing with yourself since we last met? Some, yeah. I confess; I've been keeping an eye on you.' She rose to accept two ceramic mugs from a secretary, handed one to me. 'But do I know what you're doing here? Why you've decided to come see me today? Not at all. I'm hoping that perhaps you have what our lieutenant likes to call a crisis of conscience and are here to unburden yourself of whatever guilt has been bothering you since you withheld evidence in a police investigation.'

'What makes you think that?' I sipped. The coffee tasted like warm river water, not one of the nice rivers, maybe the Passaic.

'It happens,' she explained. 'Decent people, middle class rule followers – like yourself – lie or withhold information, but you can't stomach the guilt for long. It gets under your skin; you know? Gets in the folds and wrinkles of your clothes, doesn't leave you alone.'

I waited, anticipating more.

'Am I right?'

'No,' I said. 'I'm not here to unburden myself.'

'Oh, really?' Clearly, she didn't believe me.

'No, I'm here to pass on information I hope will help lead you to Mrs. Werner's killer. As a matter of fact, I'm almost certain it will. And while you might believe that I withheld this information during our last conversation, I . . . disagree.'

'You disagree? That's delightful. Perhaps we'll let the county attorney's office decide whether or not they *agree*.' She added unnecessary emphasis just to be a bitch.

I back pedaled. 'Do I need a lawyer this time?'

'You came to me, Mr. Edwards.'

'You didn't answer the question.'

She hesitated, just a beat, sipped from her mug. Nodding, she found a pen and a sloppy legal pad, the page corners rolling up. 'I'll tell you what; we can talk all you like about material witnesses and evidence in my investigation as long as –'

'As what?' I cut her off, regretted appearing so anxious.

'As long as we agree that for at least part of our meeting we're going to discuss this game of business card roulette you seem to have been playing for the past . . . oh, fifteen years, I think. That sound about right to you? Fifteen?'

Light in Siegrist's office dimmed; my throat tried to close. I gulped a mouthful of acrid coffee just to keep from choking to death on my own stupidity. The chair, uncomfortable on its best day, threatened to ensnare me forever in this inhospitable room. 'So . . . I need a lawyer.'

Siegrist gave this honest consideration. 'Actually, I don't think so. I'm waiting for a response from the county attorney's office if there's anything we can make stick. But not kidding, I don't believe there is. Sure, there are laws regarding inciting mayhem or riots and violating confidentiality and impersonating others to their detriment, but nothing that fits your particular brand of bad behavior. Honestly, I think you're more at risk of civil litigation, if word of your exploits ever reaches any of your offended parties.'

'How did you . . .' Never having been interrogated by the police, I had no idea when the *right to remain silent* became good advice.

Now Siegrist laughed. 'I'll tell you; *that* was a goddamned chore. I've uncovered evidence of six cases that came through this office in the past fifteen years, but I'm sure that's not nearly the extent of them. The system of cross referencing and keyword searching I did was only as effective as the degree of accuracy and description of the case details filed by the investigating or arresting officers. And to be honest . . . those aren't always the most accurate or thorough by any means. Cops are, by nature, not the most thorough or talented writers. Details get left off reports, especially after the fact . . . a couple of days later . . . when key evidence in the warrant, the arrest, and the prosecutor's case has been documented.'

'I don't understand,' I said, and meant it. 'What details? What are you talking –'

Siegrist interrupted. 'Oh, little things like a city official's fingerprint match on a business card located at the scene, especially when the card itself provided the impetus for the arrest.' She grinned at me over her coffee mug. 'Oops.'

I wanted to punch her in the face. 'I still don't –'

'C'mon, Edwards. You didn't come all the way down here to bullshit me. You were fingerprinted seventeen years ago when you went to work for the city planner's office.' She drew a makeshift diagram of two stick figures, one holding a pretend gun. 'Person A assaults and batters Person B. Most of the time, not kidding 99% of the time, that's all we need. People are high; they're drunk. They confess after a few hours in the tank, or fifteen people witness the whole thing. We get statements, hand it all over to lawyers who negotiate plea bargains, and the wheels of justice turn another quarter of an inch.' She added an X to the pretend gun, then doodled quickie handcuffs on Bad Stickman. 'Rarely, almost never, does the fingerprint of an uninvolved, otherwise innocent, nowhere-near-the-scene city planner matter in closing the case.'

'But –'

'Doncha just love *buts*?' She grinned again, enjoying herself. '*But* every now and then a cop-wanna-be novelist will add a reference to the business card or the fingerprint, just to be thorough. A lot of the time it's a younger cop, not yet . . . you know . . . sure about what to document and what to leave out.'

'So you've been connecting the dots on my . . . business cards? Looking into old cases? Why?'

'It started as a keyword search and a print search I ran in our database, got three hits right out of the gate. The first was your public works print, yawn, but the other two were cases that shouldn't have had any connection to you at all. One was a domestic dispute ending in facial reconstruction surgery for a woman from Ocean County. Apparently, she'd been caught with an incriminating message from her lover on the windshield of her SUV. The other was a road rage case in which a jealous boyfriend rammed an El Camino repeatedly into the back of a van owned by a plumber who'd never heard of Mr. El Camino's girlfriend, never met her, never slept with her, nothing.'

I didn't respond, but remembered both cards clearly. The woman in the SUV had cut in front of me to take the last parking space at the mall one Christmas Eve, so I left a note from her lover. I can't remember which card I used, but her husband or boyfriend must have discovered it and beaten the shit out of her. The El Camino had changed lanes abruptly one morning when Maggie and I were taking Danny to breakfast. Maggie slammed on the brakes and skidded into the curb. Danny hit his head on the window, needed just a butterfly bandage, but it pissed me off. So I confessed to nailing El Camino's girlfriend seven ways to Sunday. I left it on a business card from the same plumber who'd screwed me on the leaky toilet (and then Maggie on a dry motel bed).

Jesus Christ, it worked. I never believed it would actually lead to people getting hurt.

Siegrist read my mind, knew I was fairly well steeped in self-loathing. So she kept going, 'The rest took some serious digging on my part, and I'm sure I missed a few, but the ones I found or think I found . . . well, they're some pretty impressive work. You're like the anti-Cupid of Train Wrecks, Divorces, and Domestic Disputes. Your photo ought to be on the wall at the county lockup.'

'So you don't believe I killed Mrs. Werner.' I stated this, didn't ask. 'Otherwise, we wouldn't be here with you making fun of me.'

'Now, don't skip to the end. We're getting there.'

'But the red pickup, the Ford. You know about the Ford. Obviously.'

'I do,' Siegrist flipped through a few pages, explaining the sloppy rolled corners. 'But I also know about Harold Cargill, hardware store manager, assaulted outside his place of business by James Worthington, an assistant football coach at Manalapan High School. I know about Sondra Baines who was married to Mark O'Brian, but who killed herself (carbon monoxide in their garage while her kids watched *SpongeBob*) when she learned of Mark's alleged homosexual affair with Thomas Freiburg. You were especially creative on that one. However, I'm also thinking it's that one that'll cost you the most in civil court – should any of this leak.'

Ligaments, tendons, muscle, I don't know what it was . . . whatever's in there . . . tightened in my chest. I pressed the flat of my palm against my ribcage, just pressed, hoping to loosen my infrastructure enough that I didn't fall over dead on the scuffed tiles of Siegrist's checkerboard floor. 'We're done here, Detective. This isn't fun. This isn't entertain –'

'No! It isn't!' She slapped her own palm hard on the desk, splashing a dollop of coffee on her notes. 'But we're not done, Mr. Edwards. Almost. But not quite.'

I sucked in a few stabilizing breaths. Waited.

'I know about Maria Georgina. Remember her?'

Another breath, slowly. 'No.'

'It seems that she received a card outside a hair dresser in Belmar. I don't have the first clue what you were doing at a hair dresser in Belmar, but different strokes and all that. Anyway, Maria decided that she didn't like the note from Martin Foster, assistant manager of the supermarket over on Cedar Road. So she set his house on fire one morning before his kids left for school.'

I muttered. 'Jesus, Jesus.'

'Oh, they were fine. The Fosters got the kids out, even saved the dog, but the house and all of their possessions were lost, and young Ms. Georgina – who has anger management issues, I'll grant you that – received a seven-to-ten spot in Trenton for arson. She'll be out in four if she behaves herself.'

I had enough. My face wet with nervous sweat, I drank more coffee just to have something useful to do. 'The red Ford . . . he's been leaving me messages, Werner's business cards, the same message –'

'Where are they? These cards?'

'Well, I don't . . . I didn't keep them. I know that's stupid, but that pickup, it's been all over me for the past month. Every time I turn around –'

'You're all worked up about that truck.'

'How do you know about it? How could you know?'

'The SVT? The big bastard, that fire engine red monstrosity? Yeah, that pickup is owned by Karl Allan Werner.'

I dropped my mug; it shattered on the checkerboard floor. 'Werner?'

Ignoring the puddle of shards, Siegrist stared me down. 'Karl Allan Werner is the reason I came to visit you in the first place. He's the reason I started digging into old cases, odd marriages between strange bedfellows determined to stab, beat or dismember one another all thanks to your business card trick or treating. Karl Werner is Alfrieda Werner's son.'

'Her . . . son?'

'And he didn't kill his mother.' Siegrist allowed this to sink in. 'His alibi is better than yours.'

I rose to leave, the wooden chair groaning in protest. 'I'm . . . I'm gonna go. I'm . . .'

'You should stay,' Siegrist stood as well. 'We have lots to talk about.'

Two steps from the door, I turned. 'Am I . . . am I a suspect? Am I under arrest?'

'Yes and no.'

'Yes and no?'

'Yes, you're a suspect, but no, you're not under arrest. You have a pretty solid alibi for the night Werner was killed. You were seen by a dozen or more people at the soccer game, at dinner afterward, and in the hotel lobby headed for your room before lights out.'

'So how can I be a suspect?'

Siegrist smirked. There's no better word for it. She smirked, as if amused at sharing something in an official context that we both already knew. 'Security footage at the Pine Ridge Motel in Atlantic County caught dozens of people, literally dozens, moving in and out of the lobby between the hours of midnight and 4:00 a.m. Who knew that many people are up and around all night long?'

'However . . .'

'Right,' she nodded. 'Exactly none of them were you.'

'And yet I'm still under suspicion for a murder that took place 40 miles away?'

'Well, there's also a security camera on the motel's side door. It's not the best set of images, and they probably wouldn't make a difference in court, because any lawyer worth a pinch of raccoon shit can create all kinds of doubt.'

'Which is why you're telling me about them.'

'You're not stupid, Edwards.' Siegrist gestured to the chair. I grudgingly sat back down. 'Two people exited the motel by that side door early Sunday morning. One was a young woman at about 12:20 a.m. who was either too drunk or too stupid to realize that she was leaving without pants. That must've been awkward or maybe a great party. I dunno.'

'And?'

'And at 1:43 a.m., someone wearing a Monmouth Galaxy soccer jacket and running gloves went out that way. From the overall shape and stature, we think it's a man, but we can't be certain. The logo is fairly clear; the rest of the image . . . meh, not so much.'

'And you think it's me? It can't be me. I . . . I went to breakfast in the lobby with my son before his first game. I had awful scrambled eggs, wet hash browns, orange juice. Danny ate . . . I can't remember, but I know he went running that morning, just a quick jog, got back before breakfast. Hell, he even did laundry!'

Siegrist raised her hands to calm me down. 'It's not time for your defense, Edwards. When . . . *if* . . . we have that conversation, your lawyer will tell you what to say and when to say it.'

'You said I was still a suspect.'

'I did.'

'How's that possible? How'd I get back into the motel? Isn't there security footage of me sneaking back in?'

'That's one we're not discussing today.'

'Why not?'

'Because of all the outrageous nonsense you've been slinging my way for the past couple of months, that particular question is one for which I might want a serious answer.'

'But . . .'

Again, she cut me off. Her face flushed; an unsightly vein bulged in her forehead. 'But nothing. Karl Werner didn't kill his mother. He's not been sending you business cards, and I'm sick to frigging death of you wasting my time with lies and misdirection.' She rose to escort me out. 'I'll be in touch if we need to speak again, sir. Until then, knock off the business cards, or I'm going to bury what's left of you in an abandoned refrigerator outside Newark. Understand?' Without warning, she'd modulated from relaxed amiability to ugly brutality and accomplished it in one breath. Looming over me, Siegrist added, 'I'm sorry, Mr. Edwards; I didn't hear you.'

I smelled tangy anger through those off-the-rack clothes. 'Yeah, all right, no more cards.'

'And here,' she scrawled something I couldn't read on a piece of letterhead. 'Call me if you have another crisis of conscience. The investigation is ongoing.'

Danny arrived home in tears an hour later. Someone had thrown a brick through his front window and defecated – yeah, took a shit – on the front seat of his car. He was so distraught about it that he didn't notice the business card beneath his windshield wiper.

ROBERT MORRIS HIGH SCHOOL
ALFRIEDA WERNER
Mathematics Instructor/Department Chair

And sketched on the back in that same wandering cursive: *TELL DADDY TO LEAVE THE POLICE OUT OF THIS.*

I needed two hours to calm him down. A pizza, three Diet Cokes, a bottle of wine for me, and two episodes of *The Walking Dead* later, he finally came around. 'Dad, aren't you gonna call the police?'

'Yeah,' I lied. 'I'll get to it soon. Wanna make sure you're okay first. They'll probably send someone over to the school to check their security footage. Vandalism. It's an awful thing to do to a guy, but we both know you don't really have any enemies. Right?'

'No one,' he agreed. 'I mean, yeah, there are some guys around who are assholes to everyone, but nothing special with me. You know? They're just ugly bullies. They pick on . . . I dunno, everybody.'

I shrugged pretend nonchalance. 'See? That's probably what it is. Just a couple of jackasses being jackasses. The principal and the security guys can check the cameras back there, find anyone who might have been around.' I pressed him, just a little. 'Did you see anyone? Anything out of the ordinary? Some of these bully muscleheads, they drive . . . well, in my day they all drove big trucks. Any badass pickups out there?'

'Nah, nothing like that.' Seemingly calm now, he flipped through channels, only half listening.

'Weren't there a bunch of kids and coaches hanging around?'

'It was my fault,' he explained. 'I forgot my math book in my locker, had to shower after practice, then get the janitor to let me through the gate so I could get upstairs. By the time I got back down, almost everyone was gone. The parking lot was pretty empty.'

'Actually,' I pretended to be heartened by this news, 'that's even better. It'll make it easier for them to find out who's on the video tape.'

While I didn't confess as much to my son, somehow I knew that corner of the parking lot, out by the practice fields, would be just a bit too far away, too far to the left, too goddamned *something* to capture a useful image on tape. I knew it.

So when Danny got distracted by another round of Georgia zombies, I sneaked upstairs.

I'd never been good with a gun, had only fired this one about fifteen times. The day I bought it, the sales guy insisted I accompany him out back, tug on a pair of unflattering earmuffs, and shoot wildly toward a hay bale with a target in the shape of a shoulderless man or a boobless woman. I think I hit Shoulderfree Sam two or three times – it might have been twenty feet away – and left feeling safer about in-home security.

If I didn't manage to kill or even injure a home intruder, the $675 handgun, a .357 magnum (not kidding, because it's fun to say at cocktail parties) made such a frigging racket that I'd scare the boogers out of any garden variety burglar while also alerting the entire neighborhood. And no one would have to get hurt.

I found the gun where I'd hidden it after my divorce, in a shoebox filled with bits of otherwise sentimental silliness: love letters, ticket stubs, restaurant checks, and assorted oddments that reminded me I'd once been happily married to the Frankenstein monster.

I opened the spinny bullet holder thing – yeah, I'm deadly – discovered the same six shells I loaded in there fifteen years ago, and snapped it closed like I'd seen Dirty Harry do in dozens of movies.

I felt better. It nearly distracted me from the very real possibility that I might have to shoot someone before dawn. Tucking the gun, pistol, whatever, into my back pocket, I returned downstairs to watch Rick Grimes shoot zombies in the head repeatedly from 75 feet away, shots I couldn't make with Lasik surgery and a month's practice.

Danny stood in the kitchen, reading over Detective Siegrist's letterhead.

'Dad,' he waved the page at me. 'What's this?'

Think of a lie. Think of a lie. Think of a lie.

'Dad?'

'Um . . . that's a note from a friend of mine who needed me to have her cell number. I didn't have my phone with me this afternoon, so she –'

'Siegrist?' He didn't give a shit about my explanation. 'Is that Kerri Siegrist's mom? I heard she's a cop. Is she the one you talked to when we went to the station that time? Could you call her about my car? That would be easy. I mean, she was at the school tonight.'

I froze halfway across the living room. 'What?'

'I dunno if this is Kerri's mom.'

'No, no,' I pointed a finger, gesturing forward in time. 'After that.

What did you say after that?'

'She was at school tonight. Mrs. Siegrist. She's cool. She's a cop for the city or the county. I dunno. Her daughter plays for Morris. She's on Galaxy, too. 18-U though. She's a year older than me.'

'Kerri . . .'

'Siegrist, yeah. She's a badass, committed to . . . UPenn, I think. Or maybe it's Pitt. But she's been stressed out lately, because she's flagging math.'

'Wait. What?'

'Yeah, her mom was great back in the day . . . that's what I hear, was gonna be a star at Southern Cal or UCLA, someplace, but she tanked some classes senior year, lost it all, had to play at Monmouth.'

My knees threatened to give way. Sitting heavily, I collapsed onto my sofa, thankful the .357 didn't blow half my ass off in the process. My mind engaged in a tug-of-war with itself. *Siegrist has a daughter who plays for the women's 18-U Manalapan Galaxy? Siegrist has a daughter . . . named Kerri? She attends Robert Morris High School.* And while I knew the answer to my next question, I asked anyway: 'Danny . . .'

'Dad? You okay?' He sat beside me, Siegrist's nasty missive still in his hand. 'Dad?'

'Danny, who does Kerri Siegrist have for math?'

'Advanced Math/Trig . . . um, yeah, she had Werner. So she's got the same long-term sub as the rest of us now, Moulen. He's good.'

She failed me . . . . Advanced Math. I had to make it up in night school . . . was a bitch, even back then . . .

'And Kerri's gonna play soccer for Pitt? UPenn?'

'Not if she doesn't bring up that math grade.' He tried forcing a laugh but couldn't. Danny understood how hard year-round soccer players work to connect with college coaches. Having one grumpy math teacher screw things up at the eleventh hour just wasn't funny – not to her, not to her teammates.

And not to her mother.

Danny went up to bed about an hour later. I washed dishes and stuffed the pizza box into our recycling bin. I swept the kitchen, hung damp dish towels, tossed trash bags into the garage, then watched CNN for thirty minutes, all just killing time until he fell asleep.

I checked on him, my seventeen-year-old son, like I might have when he was seventeen months.

He lay in bed, sleeping peacefully, entirely unaware that a killer, perhaps a police detective killer, might be on her way to our house right now.

Downstairs, I compared the writing on the most recent card: *TELL DADDY TO LEAVE THE POLICE OUT OF THIS* with the note Siegrist handed over right before kicking me out of her office: *CALL ME IF YOU*

HAVE ANOTHER CRISIS OF CONSCIENCE.

By 2:40 a.m., I figured Siegrist wasn't going to show up and kill us. I hoped I wouldn't hear Werner's carnivorous pickup rumble into my driveway, and I'd eaten the last of our pizza, three unnecessary slices I already regretted. With the .357 on the placemat beside me, I read over Siegrist's note and the business card again, again, for the sixty-eighth time, and again.

They were close. The *E*'s in *LEAVE* and *POLICE* sort of matched the *E*'s in *CONSCIENCE* and *ME*. The *T*'s also lined up nicely, but the *A*'s didn't match worth a damn.

What convinced me were the double *L*'s in *TELL* and *CALL.*

. . . someone wearing a Monmouth Galaxy soccer jacket and running gloves went out that way. From the overall shape and stature, we think it's a man, but we can't be certain.

'Overall shape and stature, Detective?' I swilled more wine. 'It's you. You knew that camera was there, just posed for your blurry snapshot. Didn't you?'

And I confess: At 3:26 a.m., I had a crisis of conscience. It's the sort of thing one can confess in the strange hours of early morning. I'd had some troubling episodes that led to significant anger with my ex-wife after her infidelity. Granted, I never beat her or tossed her down a flight of stairs, but I wanted to – pretty badly – from time to time. I managed to get past it, but she and her lawyer used my anger against me in court. It's why Danny and I ended up living in a split-level ranch with less than 2,000 finished square feet and almost no back yard.

But at 3:26 a.m., I collected Siegrist's letter, begrudgingly climbed the stairs to my bedroom, and flipped on the light in my closet. The shoe box where I'd hid my .357 still sat on the floor. I took a seat, plopped my wine glass and my handgun on the carpet, and rooted around inside the box.

I found them: two love letters I'd written to Maggie when we were in college.

I'd used my script, the same looping cursive I learned from Monmouth County's finest elementary teachers.

And it was spot-on.

Not only did the double-*L*'s match the business card, but the *A*'s were a dead-frigging bull's eye as well. The *E*'s were off, not nearly as close as Siegrist's, but all in all, the evidence against me nearly matched the evidence against her.

Is it you? Did you do all of this to yourself? Just another string of episodes?

I drank the rest of my wine, gulped it, wiped my face pointlessly with one hand.

Have you been imagining all of this? Even that frigging truck?

No.

No. You didn't kill Mrs. Werner.

Right?

Rising from the narrow carpeted floor, I tossed the box of memories into the corner and took my gun and my wine downstairs to sleep on the couch. Convinced – nearly, sort of convinced – that Detective Siegrist had beaten Alfrieda Werner to death and then used my history of business card roulette as a means to distract investigators from evidence linking her to the killing, I didn't sleep well. With every click, groan, creak, and shudder my house made as the refrigerator, the heat, or the ice maker switched on, I opened my eyes, awaiting the inevitable knock.

How would she do it? Would she shoot me then plant evidence to convict me after the fact?

Would she shoot Danny? No way. Not a mother with a soccer player in high school.

Not a mother, a murderer.

I needed to force the whole interchange outside, away from Danny. Maybe on my lawn with neighbors watching she wouldn't be able to trump up some bullshit excuse to blow my brains out. Although, confronting her with a loaded .357 in my pocket was arguably a stupid course of action. I slipped the gun from my pocket and left it on the detective's scribbled letterhead beside my empty wine glass.

Later, I remembered seeing the swamp green clock on my microwave, 4:12 a.m.

I saw it again at 5:19, when the hammering began. The wine and pizza fog lifted slowly as I rose from the stupor that had swaddled me an hour earlier.

I half imagined Danny upstairs. 'Dad?'

'. . . the door, Edwards! This is Detective Janet Siegrist of the Monmouth County Prosecutor's Office. We are here with a warrant for –'

'What?' I rolled to my side, nearly tumbled from the sofa. The hammering continued. 'Shit . . . what? Hold on?'

Again: 'Dad?'

'Hold on . . . hold on!' I tried shouting, failed. 'Danny?' Pressing myself up, I lurched for the door, cleared phlegm from my throat. 'Yeah, hang on. I'm here. Hang on.' I felt as much as heard Danny on the stairs behind me. 'Back to your room, buddy. Please. I'll be done here in a minute.'

'But Dad –'

I opened the door and immediately had a uniformed officer, Monmouth County Sheriff's Department, then another, press into the room, guns drawn. One waved an official looking document in my face while the other gripped my upper arm and forced me backwards against the door jam. A third officer followed; each outfitted in a Kevlar vest and MCSD jacket. All three shouted rowdy orders into my face. I still have no idea what they said.

Detective Siegrist entered last. My rage warmed considerably at the sight of her in a protective vest with a badge dangling from a length of rawhide about her neck, just below the gold *27* pendant.

Kerri's soccer number; it's gotta be.

Above the shouting and threats, I watched her lips move, something official and legally required, no doubt, as she withdrew a folded document from her jacket.

Time slowed. Somewhere, in a boring, predictable corner of the universe, my ice maker clicked on; my heat turned off. My house groaned, and my son slept peacefully, oblivious and safe in his room. No one threatened him with guns. No one held his father immobile against the wall, and no one shouted riotous directives while waving incoherent judicial paperwork.

Finally, I heard him. Standing confused and frightened beside the coffee table, he ignored the police, looked to me. 'Dad, I remembered the cursive. Did you see the cursive?' And Danny reached for my gun.

One of the officers pinning me to the wall turned on him. The momentary distraction, just that instant, was enough for some primitive parental instinct buried in my DNA to explode into fierce action. Shoving the first officer, I took two steps toward my son, shouted, 'No, Danny! No!' and dove, hoping to tackle him before Detective Siegrist and her kangaroo posse emptied their semi-automatics into his frail, still frail, still seventeen-month-old-and-sleeping-peacefully-upstairs body. Airborne, I cleared the back of the couch, reaching, shielding him, hoping to swallow him up, use my shoulders, back, head, anything to protect him from the barrage of bullets.

In a heartbreaking moment before landing bodily on him, I read the truth in Danny's face, saw him mouth the word *cursive.*

And we were rolling in a heap across the carpet.

I heard, then felt the first two shots, pinpricks in my shoulder and lower back, almost imperceptible. Days later, I learned that there were eleven more before Siegrist put a stop to the slaughter.

Miraculously, only two of those eleven managed to hit Danny, one in his lower rib cage causing his lung to collapse and several pints of blood to empty into his abdomen. The other struck him below his left knee, not life threatening, but clearly ending any hope he had of playing Division I soccer.

A team of vascular surgeons at Freehold Medical Center were able to save his life, inflate his lung and suture his tissues. But no amount of surgery would ever see him regain his skills on the soccer pitch.

A lunatic jumble of memories from that morning have stuck with me but never arranged themselves into anything that makes sense. There were more shouts, plenty of shoving, pushing, and rolling, handcuffs for me and Danny, lots of static sounds through multiple radios, sirens, paramedics, needle injections, foggy, stuporous bouts of extreme difficulty concentrating, bubbles of foamy blood bursting on my son's lips, and one muffled cry, just a mix of slippery vowels melted together then shouted. I'll remember that forever, the sound Danny made when shot nearly to death in my living room.

I woke some time later in what must have been surgical recovery, the room about me beeping and exhaling in a Vaderesque adagio. I tried lifting my head, struggled, then rested it back on the gurney. 'Who's there?'

Siegrist rose at the edge of my vision. Hazy and indistinct, she tried telling me something.

'Where's my son?'

'. . . still in surgery,' she leaned close to keep eye contact. '. . . need you to understand . . . remanded into custody . . . calling your wife . . .'

I summoned what clarity I could, drew half a breath, 'Piss off. You're a murderer.'

'. . . Edwards . . .' she morphed and slid about as if through a smeary film of water.

'Stay away from him.'

When I woke again, I was in a hospital room; I have no idea how much later. No one occupied the bed beside me, but Detective Siegrist sat reading from her legal pad, jotting notes into a case file.

I tried moving, found that I could shift around pretty well, except for my left arm, which rested in some traction apparatus obviously designed to keep it elevated and immobile. Thirsty, I looked for water but didn't find anything, no flowers, presents, chocolates, or get well cards. I closed my eyes against the incandescent glare, and croaked. 'You're a murderer.'

I heard Siegrist stand. 'Well . . . look who's awake. How are you feeling, Mr. Edwards?'

'You killed Werner,' I said, 'because you were pissed off about your daughter's scholarship. And now you're gonna make it look like I did it.'

'You didn't do it,' she said. 'Your son did, broke his own windshield, even dropped a load in his own car.'

'Get out of here,' I tried to sound as angry as I felt. 'Get me a lawyer.'

'You don't need a lawyer,' Siegrist explained. 'Danny does. And your ex-wife already got him one.'

'You have no material evidence against him,' I threatened. 'You're gonna get sued.'

She cocked an eyebrow. 'Oh, really?'

'Yeah, sued. I'll be all over you, your supervisors, the county, all of you pricks.'

'Is Danny missing a watch? An Ironman running watch?'

My heart ground to a rusty stop; I used post-surgical confusion to mask my terror. 'I dunno. Who cares?'

'And how about those soccer shoes? Size thirteen. That's some pair of canoes, Edwards. He's got big feet, a growing boy, no doubt.' Her voice modulated into some jackass impersonation of Red Riding Hood's grandmother, *'The better to leave footprints in an old lady's flowerbeds, dearie.'*

'So what. Lots of guys wear thirteens. I do.' Noting Siegrist's easy confessions, I wondered if she had more. Probably, but nothing she'd admit; she was too smart for that. A bloody, broken watch and a clutch of muddy footprints stung. I had to admit, but they wouldn't bury Danny, not if I could help it. 'Shove off. Leave me alone. You broke into my house.'

'Suit yourself,' she said, 'but think about it. Why would your son go jogging the morning after playing two soccer games when he knows he has at least two more to play? Who does that?'

I struggled to adjust my shoulders and neck. The Spanish inquisitorial torture device kept one side of me from moving at all. 'That doesn't make him a killer.'

'I have video tape of him entering the hotel after his jog . . . without a watch.'

'So?'

'But no video of him ever leaving.' She reached to help as I adjusted my shoulders and pillow.

'Don't touch me!'

'It was Danny who left the hotel at 1:43 that morning. He took your car, drove to Alfrieda Werner's home, and beat her to death. He wore running gloves to avoid leaving prints, drove back, ran around the block a few times, then entered the hotel in a sweaty t-shirt with a plastic baggie of bloody warmups in his hand.'

'Nonsense.'

'You said yourself that he did laundry that morning. Did you ever stop to wonder why? What teenage soccer player gives a shit if his warmup is a little smelly on day two of a tournament?'

'Where'd he get the business cards? Werner's cards?'

Siegrist shrugged. 'He might have taken them that night, which is unlikely given that he didn't know about your business card game until he met with Detective Carlisle a week later. So I'm guessing he lifted them from her classroom. The assistant principal noted that she had a stack of cards on her desk, but there were none in the box of effects that Carlisle and I delivered to Karl Werner after the autopsy. Danny might have sneaked into her room; hell, he might've helped the AP box up Werner's shit. Who knows?'

'Why? What motive did he have to kill her?' I blinked several times in an effort to get Siegrist into focus, didn't want to say anything incriminating. I understood that this conversation wouldn't be admissible as evidence against my son, but still, it wouldn't do Danny's case any good for me to pass along potential leads to an investigating officer. I tried dragging her in another direction. 'You had more motive to kill Werner than my son. What's UPenn cost these days? Seventy? Seventy-five thousand? That's a lot of scholarship to lose over a trig grade.'

Siegrist ignored me. 'Danny's a year-round soccer player, headed to a DI commitment. He's got five Advanced Placement classes this year and a 3.96 GPA. Jesus, Edwards, the kid's a frigging star.'

'Yeah? So?'

'That's a lot of pressure on one kid . . . on any kid with that kind of load, especially in the wake of such a nasty divorce, having to move in with you, only seeing Mom on weekends. These kids today, competing for scholarships, they gotta have the academics, athletics, leadership, community service, SAT scores, all kinds of bullshit we didn't worry about thirty years ago.'

'I still don't see how that makes him a killer.'

'Kids snap. We see it all the time. He reached for the gun; it was a suicide. We both know it.'

'No. Get lost,' I said. 'We're done talking.'

She turned to go. 'That's fine. We can speak again later, when you're feeling up to it. But just two things to think about while you rest . . .'

'What?'

She gathered up her legal pad, notes, and the file folder. 'What do you think he meant when Danny said *I remembered the cursive*? You heard him; right? What do you suppose he was confessing with that comment?'

'Eat shit.'

She pressed on. 'And ask yourself: After meeting with Carlisle, did Danny ever mention your games of business card roulette? I'm betting he didn't. Why might that be? Huh?'

'You're lying. Carlisle didn't say anything to him. Now, get out.'

She nodded, then left.

Two days passed before they released Danny from the ICU. A nurse wheeled me up to his room; my traction device conveniently attached to the wheelchair's armrest, so my shoulder could remain elevated.

I waited until my ex-wife and Danny's lawyer left that afternoon, then rolled in. He was groggy, but awake, looking pale, drawn, beaten. Immediately I wanted to take him someplace warm with pleasant sun, deep fried seafood and onshore breezes, someplace he could convalesce in quiet comfort – not this frigging concrete tomb. He saw me and smiled. 'Hey, Dad.'

Nope. Not ever. Never could I believe that this boy was a murderer. And if he was, fine, screw it: he's a murderer. Maybe the miserable old witch had it coming.

I rolled close to his bed. 'Hey, buddy. How you feeling?'

'Like warm dogshit.'

'Lovely,' I said, 'but don't say "dogshit." It's not a nice word.'

He laughed, then winced. 'Don't be funny. It makes my lung bleed.'

'Okay, no laughing.' It was then that I noticed the handcuff. Familiar, comforting rage tried to boil over, but I beat it back. It wouldn't do Danny any good. 'They at least keeping you comfortable?'

'Not bad,' he said. 'I ate today. Meatloaf, I think.'

'I had that, too,' I said, 'thought it was Jell-O. Wasn't I surprised?'

He laughed again, 'Dad!'

'Sorry!'

He drew a long breath that seemed to hurt near the end, then exhaled slowly with only the faintest hint of a frothy, bubbling wheeze. I identified it as another mortal enemy; that wheeze had to go. He whispered, 'They say I killed Mrs. Werner.'

Did you? You can tell me. I swear to God you can. Just whisper it; just nod, and I'll go down with you. I swear.

'Yeah, I heard,' I said. 'And I know that's gotta be terrifying, but I don't want you to worry about it now.'

He rattled the handcuff against the bed frame. 'That's a bit hard to do. You know?'

'Try,' I said. 'Your mom and I . . . there's no way we believe you did it, Danny. No –'

He interrupted. 'Mom thinks I did. She's already working with the attorney on my defense, figures they might get some kind of plea or something. I didn't understand all of it.'

Of course she does. Of goddamn course.

'Danny,' I decided to jump in head first. 'I need to ask you . . . that morning, when you came downstairs, you said *I remembered the cursive*. What did you mean? Everything happened so fast. You reached for the gun, and then . . . well, here we are.'

He shook his head. His eyes closed. 'I didn't reach for the gun. I was reaching for that paper, the piece of paper Kerri's mom had written on. She wrote it in cursive.'

'Yeah? So what?'

'So it was just like the cursive that night in the parking lot of the grocery store. Remember that card? The business card from the stranger who didn't like your parking job . . . that was in cursive, too, just like the card on my car the other night. I remembered, was trying to show you.'

'You weren't reaching for the gun?'

'Why would I reach for a gun? The gun was on the coffee table with the piece of paper.'

Siegrist, I'm gonna kill you. I swear to God. I'm gonna bash your goddamned brains out.

I needed only one question answered to know — *to believe, almost believe* — that my son was innocent. He seemed to sleep; I didn't want to disturb him but I'd lose my mind if I didn't ask. 'Danny?'

He stirred, didn't open his eyes. 'Huh?'

'Buddy, why did you deliver all those cards to me? Was that some kind of punishment? Were you angry about me and your mom? Just needed some revenge?'

'Cards?' His eyes fluttered then fell closed again. 'I didn't deliver any cards.'

I watched him sleep fifteen minutes before making up my mind. Embracing the rage, finally, I let it have me, just gave myself up. Maybe I'd track down Siegrist, Werner, and (hopefully) my NAZI-whore ex-wife in Hell.

I found a copy of the yellow pages in Danny's bedside cabinet. Twenty-six car rental agencies served greater Monmouth County. At three minutes each, I figured I might get lucky and have my answer inside of an hour.

If you screwed up, Siegrist. Just one irretrievable screw up.

I started with the first on the list: A-1 Auto Rentals.

'Hi, my name is Dale Siegrist. I'm hoping you can help me out. I'm trying to reconcile a confusing charge on my VISA from last month when my wife, Janet, rented . . . um, I think it was a truck, a pickup, a big one. I can't remember the exact make and model. Anyway, she said she didn't take the optional insurance, but my credit card statement looks like she did. Do you think you can help me?'

I waited less than a minute while the receptionist searched the A-1 Auto Rentals database and confirmed for me that Janet Siegrist hadn't rented anything from them in the past month.

'That's fine,' I apologized. 'My fault. Thanks for your time. I'll figure it out.'

On to the next listing: Autos & More Rental Agency.

Again, I dialed. 'Hi, my name is Dale Siegrist, and I'm hoping you can help me out . . .'

Thirty-four minutes later, I had my answer.

Hospital orderlies hadn't given Danny a knife with his lunch; that made sense. Yet, they had allowed him to use a metal fork, albeit one handed.

I took it when I left him sleeping as peacefully as one could while handcuffed to the bed with a Monmouth County Sherriff's deputy standing guard outside.

The fork will have to do. I stashed it in my gown. *I'll make it work.*

Rolling clumsily into the corridor, I nodded to the deputy. 'Hey, can you do me a favor?'

He looked up from whatever magazine he'd been skimming. 'Yeah? Whaddya need, Edwards?'

'Can you get Siegrist on that radio? Ask her to meet me in my room? I've got something I need to share with her.'

The End. (One of them, anyway.)

***

Dear Reader,

I thank you for journeying this far and hope you enjoyed the story. If you're like me, reaching the end of a mystery generally means being awash in one of two emotions:

I knew it! Holmes thought he had me fooled, but I caught every sleight of hand!

Or: *This idiot buggered everything up. I want my ending!*

While the first ranks among the most satisfying feelings of the day, the second can be downright frustrating, borderline infuriating, as I consider all of the productive things I might have been doing rather than wasting the afternoon chasing after the wrong killer.

Do you ever wish you could have the alternate endings? Perhaps ignore the writer's inclination and catch one of the other suspects? Your suspect?

Yeah, me too.

If you're a mystery purist, stop reading now. Siegrist killed Werner, and we're done. Cue the curtain. If you think Danny did it, or Edwards himself . . . read on. We'll rejoin them in Danny's hospital room as Edwards asks that critical question about Alfrieda Werner's business cards.

Thanks again for stopping by. See you on the boardwalk.

Robert Scott
Haymarket, VA

***

He stirred, didn't open his eyes. 'Huh?'

'Buddy, why did you deliver all those cards to me? Was that some kind of punishment? Were you angry about me and your mom? Just needed some revenge?'

'Cards?' His eyes fluttered then fell closed again. 'I didn't deliver any cards.'

'You sure?' I said anything to keep him talking. 'Because if you did, if that . . . was you, we can talk about it, figure out some way to move on from here. I know . . . Jesus shit, I know I'm sometimes hard to talk to, but we can use this. We can, just you and me, we can figure out how to move on if we just get all the cards on the table. You know?'

One eye slitted opened. I dunno if he saw me.

'Dad, I'm gonna nap.'

'Okay. Okay,' I rested a hand on his chest, the bed sheet a complicit wall between us. 'I'll wait; I'll be here.'

'All right,' he muttered. 'Carlisle never said anything about it, Dad. I didn't know.'

And he was gone.

I watched him sleep fifteen minutes as dull, invasive truth pressed immutably into my chest. My balls crept up tight against my groin. My lips moved; I felt them, but nothing useful came out.

Finally, I whispered, just to hear myself: 'Danny, I never mentioned Detective Carlisle.'

Lamb of God, who taketh away the sins of the world, have mercy upon us.

Upon him. Have mercy upon him, for pity's sake.

Late afternoon sunlight painted Danny's floor with striped, ephemeral memories, reminding me that once upon a time I'd been a decent dad. Maggie and I had been happy. And my son hadn't been a murderer.

This is your fault, shithead. All of it.

Some primitive universal joint in my mind engaged, and I half rose, realized I couldn't, then slumped back. I had to get him away.

Mexico?

A Caribbean Island?

Canada. The bustling anonymity of Toronto. Some small apartment. What do I do for work? I don't know where our passports are. No. Can't cross with passports, have to cross somewhere else, have to cross through the woods – Maine or New York, maybe Champlain. Yeah, Champlain. Leave a trail. Make calls, hit some Internet sites – the Cayman Islands, Bonaire, Bolivia, Brazil, whatever, then head for Champlain. I can do it. We can do it.

Danny shifted with a sandpapery rustle, the unforgiving hospital bed, the bandages, the . . . handcuff. The god-fustickating handcuff. I had to get him out of the handcuff, had to find a key, a paper clip . . .

What are you, a locksmith? Jesus Christ.

. . . a break. A piss break. That's what I needed. They had to uncuff Danny to take a leak; there wasn't a bedpan in sight. They had to let him use the bathroom, and then . . . that's when, that's when I'd do it. I'd tackle the cop, taze him, frigging smash his ugly cop face through the hospital window, something, something, I'd do something, and we'd be gone.

No. Shit, shit, shit, shit.

The bed rail. I could dismantle the bed rail. That'd do it. I'd get my wallet, my keys, all the savings in my account, Danny's account, all of it, and I'd come back. A Phillips head screwdriver and a half-inch ratchet. Maybe five-eighths.

Just bring both, dumbass.

And we'd be gone. We'd wait for the deputy to wander down the hall for a Coke, to chat up some nurse in the kitchenette, sneak off for a cigarette, work the crossword, drink a coffee, take a shit, build something out of frigging Legos, and we'd slip past, down the stairs, into my car, and north.

Raw, inspired desperation ran my heart rate up, started me sweating. I breathed in gulps, quick swallows of antiseptic, recycled HVAC.

Yeah. Easy. It'll be easy.

Your son's a murderer. That's fine. Werner was an insufferable bitch, a monster. The world is better off without her, like Stalin or Milošević.

This is your fault.

Yeah, it is.

You gotta make this happen.

All at once, the room turned on me, was filled with entirely too much light. I wheeled to the blinds, twisted them closed, and sat in semi-darkness awash in an occlusion of muttery self-loathing and crisply-focused determination.

We'd run. We'd run until they killed me. Then he'd run and keep running, despite his punctured lung, his ruined leg.

I'd buy him a new watch, give him mine, let it keep time for him, running forever.

And I'd leave his mother a note, just a quick scribble: *Hey, sorry. But I couldn't let them have him.* Sure, that'd be enough. Short and sweet, something I might scrawl on the back of a business card.

***

He stirred, didn't open his eyes. 'Huh?'

'Buddy, why did you deliver all those cards to me? Was that some kind of punishment? Were you angry about me and your mom? Just needed some revenge?'

'Cards?' His eyes fluttered then fell closed again. 'I didn't deliver any cards.'

'You sure?' I said anything to keep him talking. 'Because if you did, if that . . . was you, we can talk about it, figure some way to move on from here. I know . . . Jesus shit, I know I'm sometimes hard to talk to, but we can use this. We can, just you and me, we can figure out how to move on if we just get all the cards on the table. You know?'

One eye slitted opened. I dunno if he saw me.

'Dad, I'm gonna nap.'

'Okay. Okay,' I rested a hand on his chest. 'I'll wait; I'll be here.'

'All right,' he muttered and slept.

I watched him fifteen minutes as late afternoon sunlight washed his floor with striped, ephemeral memories of better days once upon a time. My son – seventeen years or seventeen months, it didn't matter – shot, handcuffed, lung punctured, leg ruined, hope lost. Someone needed to pay.

I wanted blood, could taste it, metallic and tangy at the back of my throat. They'd shot my boy, had tried to kill him.

And for what? Because they believed he'd beaten his insidious monster of a trig teacher to death? Who cares? The world was better off without Alfrieda Werner, like Stalin or Milošević. She deserved what she got. Yes, goddamnit; she earned that bludgeoning, every frantic stroke.

I glanced at my watch, 5:27 p.m., the 7 blurry behind a ragged scratch in the cheap, plastic face. I'd gotten that scratch on a 10k run, a cross country deal Danny's soccer team sponsored two years earlier, a fund raiser. I'd fallen, slipped like a buffoon in some mud. I scraped my wrist, elbow, and watch on a rock, bled unsightly rivulets for three miles before the school nurse patched me up, shaking her head in disapproval.

5:27. I was hungry again, didn't know why. I'd eaten whateveritwas they'd served earlier. Perhaps all of this was folded together, wrapped up in an occlusion of rage, self-loathing, bloodlust, vengeance. That recipe would leave anyone ravenous.

Danny shifted with a sandpapery rustle. I wheeled to his window and twisted the blinds shut. Darkness erased the sun-washed floor. I listened to him breathe; yet the steady, comforting adagio failed to quiet my anger.

Someone needed to pay.

You know who, dumbass. You can't let them have him.

I decided to nap, at least to close my eyes, maybe slow my heartrate a few metronome clicks. With my feet propped on Danny's bed, I got comfortable in the wheelchair.

Breathing slowly, I tried to match him and waited for the rage to rinse out of my system.

It worked, sort of.

I drifted, remembering good days, the best days when Maggie and I were getting along; Danny was a toddler, seventeen months, and I was still a hero, could do nothing wrong. I'd only ever wish for that. If I ever won wishes in a carnival barker's tent, if any benevolent god could grant them, that's all I'd wish for: take me back to seventeen months – my hero days – and leave me there forever, with my old running watch keeping time.

Not yours, shithead. Look again.

I shook off dull, invasive truth, trying to screw with my happy recollections, closed my eyes tight against the sunlight sneaking between Danny's slatted window blinds.

Whenever you're ready . . .

I crossed and uncrossed my ankles, didn't want to wake him. I sat up, pressed my ass higher in the chair, used my heels to tug myself closer to his bedside, thought maybe if I could rest my calves and ankles on the mattress I might sleep for a while, just slide into nothingness with Danny's rhythmic breathing a steady, reliable backdrop, white noise to carry me up and away.

Look again.

I did.

Someone has to pay. They can't have him.

You do. You can.

Enough uninvited light filtered in; I made out my feet, still propped beside Danny's, lumpy in ghastly hospital slippers.

Size thirteen. It's time.

Time.

Time.

Reaching awkwardly across my body, I used my immobile traction hand to press the LIGHT button on my watch . . .

Look again.

. . . 5:36 p.m., the 6 smeary.

The tiny colon blinked away ten seconds until the dim blue glow faded. I pressed LIGHT again; 5:36 morphed into 5:37 p.m. Another 7, as smeary as the last, hid behind the scratch I'd picked up in that 10k.

Danny fell. He did. He fell in soupy mud, racing with his friends, slashed up his wrist, scraped his elbow, and scratched his watch. I'd been at the finish line when he crossed, his arm a bloody mess, his face alight with pride at having picked up new battle scars in the woods between the high school and the lake.

You lost your watch. Remember?

It might have been in Werner's living room, in her flower beds, maybe on the street around the corner from her house. You can't remember.

Size thirteen feet, four of them huddled together on Danny's bed.

One scraped up running watch.

Someone has to pay. They can't have him.

Hospital orderlies hadn't given Danny a knife; that made sense. Yet, they had allowed him a metal fork.

I took it when I left him sleeping as peacefully as one could while handcuffed to the bed with a Monmouth County Sherriff's deputy standing guard outside.

The fork will have to do. I'll make it work.

Before rolling clumsily into the corridor, I searched the semi-darkness and found it, knew it would be there: a business card from Danny's attorney. With a pen from the bedside table, I scribbled a quick note to Siegrist explaining how I managed to get back into the Pine Ridge Motel dipping momentarily behind a pair of long distance truckers who'd come in together around 5:45.

I unfastened Danny's watch, left it with the note propped on the edge of his dinner tray.

Once through the door, I renewed a tenacious grip on the fork beneath my robe and nodded to the deputy. 'Hey, can you do me a favor?'

He looked up from whatever magazine he'd been skimming. 'Yeah? Whaddya need, Edwards?'

'C'mere, would you? I wanna show you something.'

Robert Scott dreams of running across South Dakota, but he's only allowed three personal days each year, so he contents himself with interminable laps of Burke Lake in Fairfax, Virginia.

Yes, it's boring.

He spends all day teaching Edgar Poe stories to distracted high school students and hopes one day to win the New York City marathon. Assuming the first 15,000 finishers are disqualified, he's got a good chance of bringing home the victory.

For more lies about Robert, visit robscottbooks.com

Milton C. Johns

Don't Confuse the Law with Justice

The following short story is excerpted from the novel, *Delivery Vehicles*, due for release in the coming year. Some changes might exist between this and the final version.

As luck with have it, the Earth continued rotating on its axis, and sure enough I had to get up Thursday morning. I was getting decent sleep with my recreational Xanax regimen, and an extra bump in the morning got me through the day. I could feel the beast clawing at me though: Standing next to a wino in line at the 7-Eleven that morning and smelling the booze on his breath made me want to kiss him on the lips. Fortunately, I refrained. I asked Christy if she could just meet me at the courthouse Thursday morning because I had an early trial docket and she agreed. Sometimes she was almost like a human being. She had a lousy job as my court appointed practice monitor, but unlike me, she chose that arrangement. If I wanted to practice law, I had to put up with the bullshit.

My trial was in General District Court that morning, so I saw Christy on the second floor at the appointed time. She was engaged in an animated conversation with a female Mason County Police Officer. I barged into the conversation.

"What's up?" I asked. The officer was Amy Anders. In the foggy recesses of my plaque-dulled brain, I recalled that she was the responding officer in my case. Garden variety assault and battery, I think, but they never are garden variety it seems. I'd had a few cases with her before and recalled her as being a hard-ass. She was tall, almost as tall as me, with curly brown hair that she somehow kept in a bun. She seemed athletic and strong, with broad shoulders and veins bulging from her bare forearms.

"Screw you, Haskell," she grumbled. What, was it something I said?

Christy turned to me with an exasperated look. "Mr. Haskell, do you know Officer Anders?"

"Of course I do," I said. "The real question is, do you?"

Christy frowned a bit. "Officer Anders is my fiancée."

I know that my eyebrows shot up to my hairline because I had no poker face when it came to people outing each other.

"What's the problem, Haskell?" Anders asked. She reached to put her hand on the butt of her pistol, except it wasn't in its holster. The Sheriff of Mason County doesn't get along with the Chief of Police, so he won't let officers bring in their weapons. Can't play in the sandbox I guess.

"No problem, just surprised. Small world, isn't it?" I asked. I looked her up and down and imagined her and Christy rolling around naked in some hot but lovingly beautiful girl on girl action. Yes, I know I am a thirteen-year-old boy at heart.

"I was just finishing up my conversation with Officer Anders," Christy said, now glowering at Officer Amazon. Hee hee, Amazon…I needed to be careful or I would say that out loud.

"She doesn't let you call her by her first name either?" I was smiling from ear to ear. There is something irresistible about the angst and anger of others that gives me great pleasure as a spectator. If I can antagonize, so much the better.

"She's in uniform, in court, Mr. Haskell. It's a matter of respect."

"You may have heard that word before," Anders chimed in. Unwittingly, I had driven them back together against me. Shit.

"Frankly, I don't care what you call her," I said. "I will be cross examining her shortly."

Anders rolled her eyes. "You have the Garcia case this morning?"

"Yep, "I said. "He was one of my first clients. Been with me since he was 18."

"Jorge Garcia is a gangbanger," said Anders.

I spoke to Christy. "Not the fat guy from *Lost*, a different guy, by the way. Mr. Garcia has no gang convictions." I turned to Anders. "I know you officers like to make that stuff up about citizens when you need some highly implausible reason to conduct an unconstitutional stop and frisk, but, nonetheless, my client is no gangbanger."

"Whatever, Haskell," she said. "See you later." She turned on her heel.

I smiled. "See you in Hell."

Christy smacked me, hard, with the back of her hand. "I'll text you later!" She shouted after Anders.

Anders waved her hand without turning around.

"What was that all about," I asked. I set my briefcase down and rubbed my arm for effect. It didn't really hurt.

Christy folded her arms. "Me hitting you or me fighting with her?"

"You pick."

"I hit you because sometimes you are a gaping asshole," she said. It kinda turned me on when she cursed. I don't think I had heard her curse before! "I'm fighting with her because she changes her mind all the time."

"Compliment accepted," I picked up my briefcase and took two steps toward the hallway leading to the courtrooms. She followed. "What is she changing her mind about?"

"It's personal."

"Suit yourself if you don't want to talk about it," I picked up the pace, knew she would need almost two of her steps to keep up with one of mine.

"So what's this case about this morning?" Christy asked.

Near the courtroom door, I slowed up. I had to think about it. Was it garden variety A and B? "Actually, Mob Assault. Gang related stuff. Allegedly."

Her brow furrowed. "I thought you said you client wasn't a gangbanger."

"Of course. He's never been convicted of any gang offenses. What else would I tell a cop?"

"So is he a gangbanger?" she asked.

"This conversation is privileged, is it not?" I asked her.

"Yes," she said.

"Then, oh yeah, he's a major gangbanger, out of Woodbridge. I can't remember if he's MS-13 or Mexican Mafia or Latin Kings…too many to keep track. Anyway, Jorge and a couple of other guys are accused of beating up another gangbanger in a rival crew. The victim is locked up here anyway for something else."

"You've been representing him for a long time," Christy said.

"Yeah, about once a year I'm in court for Jorge. Possession, reckless driving, the laundry list of misdemeanors."

"And you've gotten him acquitted of everything?" Christy asked.

"Not quite everything. We've pled down to some lesser charges on occasion, but Jorge has never done a day in jail. Isn't going to do a day, as far as I'm concerned," I said.

In the courtroom, a handful of people sat around the gallery. Judge Freely would hear the case. He was wrapping up the traffic docket from the morning. Lots of well-meaning citizens pleading "guilty with explanation," finding out that that means the same as "guilty without explanation." Someone's cousin knew a guy who had a friend who told him to do that when you go to court, and that's what they do. Maybe a judge in Fairfax will cut you a break with that, but here in Mason County, guilty is guilty is guilty. Period. So unless I tell you to, don't ever fucking plead guilty.

I saw Jorge sitting in a bench near the exit. I motioned to him with my index finger, then stepped back into the hallway. Christy followed, dutifully, like a damned Yorkshire terrier underfoot, afraid she is going to miss something. We had one before Rachel left me. They're both gone now; only pee stains on the carpet as mementos. I'm not sure who left them. Heh.

Jorge came out. In his early thirties, he wore a freshly pressed grey suit with a purple shirt, black tie, and shiny black loafers. The Welch's shirt was a bit loud for court, but I couldn't complain. He was clean shaven with his black hair pulled back in a short ponytail. I would like to think he stole the ponytail look from me, but it could just as easily have been me who stole it from him. Honestly, I have no clue who wore it first.

I introduced him to Christy and he shook hands politely. "Nice to meet you, Mizz White," he said. He spoke without a hint of an accent, in case you are wondering. He had finished in the top ten percent of his class at one of those Prince William High Schools. Before he went bad.

"Nice to meet you, Mr. Garcia," she said.

"So are you ready?" I asked.

He nodded. "I am in good hands, so I am ready."

Christy looked at me. "When did you do trial prep for this case?"

I shrugged. "Jorge was in the office a couple of weeks ago and told me what happened. I'm good."

Christy frowned. She was good at that. "You didn't prep him, go over direct examination questions, witnesses, evidence, any of that?"

I shook my head. "Don't need it. Jorge and I have been through this. Jorge knows that all he has to do is tell the truth and the story will tell itself. If I put him on the stand."

Jorge smiled, "Yeah, pretty much, that's it."

Christy stammered, "How can you just walk in there to try –"

She was interrupted as Robert Marks stormed past us into the courtroom.

"You are a vile piece of shit, Haskell," he snarled.

"And good morning to you, Counselor," I called after.

Jorge placed a hand over his mouth to stifle a laugh.

"What was that all about?"

I smiled. "If I was a comic book villain, Marks would be my superhero nemesis. He's got the brains of the Hulk, the sophistication of Aquaman, and I'm pretty sure, Wonder Woman's twat. Oh, but with no superpowers."

Jorge laughed out loud at that. He loved my new material.

"Not a very charitable way to speak about a fellow officer of the court," Christy said. Her arms were folded again. She had on a smart grey suit, slacks and some black heels that could be worn in or out of bed, I guessed. Folding her arms like that was just going to wrinkle the suit.

"He's a tool," I said.

"Why is he upset?"

"Not entirely sure but I have an idea. Let's go back inside."

When we returned to the courtroom, I scanned the faces of the few folks still sitting in there. I noticed a middle aged, olive skinned couple. They wore faded, rumpled clothes and both clutched white forms. They caught my gaze, then looked away.

"Jorge, is that them?" I asked, a little bit loudly, pointing a little bit obviously.

"Yeah, that's them," he said.

"Good. This will be quick."

"Who are they?" Christy asked, in a much softer voice. Some redneck was prattling on to the Judge about how his pregnant baby momma called and told him she was drunk and needed a ride home and that was why he was caught driving on a suspended license. For the third time. Yeah, he was going to the klink for a few days of quality alone time.

"You'll see," I replied. The three of us squeezed onto a bench in the second row (first row reserved for officers and attorneys, don't ya know). Anders was sitting by herself in the front row behind the Commonwealth's counsel table.

Marks was sitting at the Commonwealth's Attorney counsel table, every few moments looking over his shoulder at me. I don't know if he hated me more than I hated him, but I kinda hoped he did.

Eventually the docket was complete and only the three of us, the middle-aged couple and Marks were left in the courtroom with Benson.

"The only case left is the Commonwealth versus Jorge Garcia," Freely pronounced it like "Whore Hay."

I stood. "*George* Garcia, yes, your honor. Mike Haskell for the Defendant."

Freely frowned. Christy stood. "Mizz White, very nice to see you again."

"Yes, your honor," she answered.

"Very well, is the Commonwealth ready to proceed?"

"Yes, your honor," said Marks, standing.

I motioned to Christy and Jorge to follow me past the bar to the Defendant's counsel table.

"Your honor, I believe there are supposed to be three other defendants." I looked around the courtroom for effect. The other three guys had been in scrapes with Jorge before; I damned well knew what they looked like.

"Your honor, the Commonwealth has nolle prossed those other cases. We will only be proceeding against Mr. Garcia," said Marks.

Jorge and Christy both looked quizzically at me; I had no answer besides a shrug.

"Your Honor, without the other three defendants, I don't know that the Commonwealth will be able to make out its prima facie case for Mob Assault. The statute requires more than one person to constitute a Mob." I really didn't know what Marks was up to. Or maybe he had just fucked up. It was sometimes hard to tell with Marks.

Marks stood again." Your Honor, the Commonwealth moves to amend the charge to Assault from Mob Assault."

I was still on my feet, and I think maybe some steam came out of my ears. Or maybe my ass, I'm not sure. "Your Honor, if the Commonwealth is going to amend the charge minutes before trial, I am going to need a continuance."

"Denied. It's an easier case for you to defend," said Freely. Uh, no, I thought. He's just trying to get off the bench in time for lunch. "We are going forward this morning. Any other preliminary matters?"

"Judge, Mr. Garcia speaks English and I believe the alleged victim, Mr. Hernandez, speaks English, but two of my witnesses I believe don't speak English." I turned to the middle-aged couple in the back of the courtroom. Jorge turned to look at them at the same time.

"Senor, Senora Hernandez, *necessites ustedes un translador*?" I asked in pretty good Spanish. Looks like I didn't need to be drunk to speak the language.

They both stood slowly, still clutching the white paper. "*Si, por favor*," Mr. Hernandez said softly.

"Your Honor, the Commonwealth objects to these witnesses," said Marks, glaring at me.

"On what grounds, Mr. Marks?" Freely asked.

"You can't object, Mr. Marks, I haven't even called them as witnesses. I just asked about a translator" I interrupted.

"These are the parents of the victim," said Marks.

Freely seemed confused. Fortunately, he hadn't yet figured out what I was up to.

"So? What's the legal basis for the objection? Looks like they were subpoenaed and they showed up. And I haven't called them yet. What's the issue?" I added.

Marks's face was reddening. He had nothing.

"Mr. Haskell?" the Judge asked me.

"Your Honor, I will proffer that I intend to use Mr. and Mrs. Hernandez to establish the whereabouts of both the complaining witness and my client." I said.

Freely turned to Marks. "Mr. Marks?"

Marks exhaled loudly. "Objection withdrawn."

I fake whispered to Marks, "You're not supposed to object to my witnesses until I call them as witnesses. It's kinda in the rules."

Freely turned to his clerk and asked her to have the Spanish interpreter sent up. He shuffled some papers then said, "Mr. Marks, your first witness? I believe the clerk said we have the complaining witness in custody for an unrelated matter."

"That's correct, Your Honor," said Marks. Freely turned to the Deputy Sheriff. "Bailiff, please bring in Mr. Hernandez."

I leaned over to Christy. "Watch this."

Marks is sloppy. If I were in his three-hundred-dollar shoes, I would ask for a Rule on Witnesses. That means anyone who is going to testify has to leave the courtroom until they are called. Keeps people from hearing other witnesses and conforming their stories. But Marks was rattled and angry and he blew it. It was a calculated gamble.

Shortly Hernandez appeared in an orange jumpsuit. He was cuffed and shackled at the wrists and ankles, and the deputy led him to the witness stand. Once he got on the stand he looked around the courtroom. As soon he sat, he looked at Marks, then over at the Defense table. Finally I saw his eyes widen as he noticed his parents in the back row. He swallowed hard. Jorge smiled at him.

Marks began his direct examination, reading from a yellow legal pad, with preliminary questions, name, address, occupation.

"Can you tell me what happened on the night of May third of this year, Mr. Hernandez?" Marks asked.

"Uh, I was at the 7-Eleven on Route 1 by the high school —"

"Was that Adams High School?" Marks interrupted.

"Yeah, by Adams," said Hernandez. "It was like 10 o'clock at night, and I was going in to get a Coke, and this car pulled in to the parking lot with four guys in it."

I shifted in my seat, hoping Christy didn't notice. It was taking a little longer than I thought.

"And then what happened?" asked Marks.

"The guys got out of the car and yelled at me, then they jumped me," said Hernandez.

"Explain to the court what you mean by them jumping you," Marks said.

"They were beating me up. They were punching and kicking me," Hernandez said. He looked briefly at Jorge, then looked away.

"What, if anything, did they say to you?" Marks asked.

"I don't remember them saying anything," said Hernandez. Marks looked up from his legal pad. That was clearly not the answer he expected.

"You don't remember what they said to you?"

"Naw, I don't. I don't remember. They probably didn't say anything."

Marks frowned.

"You're sure they didn't say anything?" he asked.

"I don't remember," said Hernandez. He was looking at his feet.

Marks glared at me. What did I do? I hate 7-Eleven.

"Did you recognize any of the men who jumped you?"

"No," said Hernandez.

Marks threw his legal pad on the table. "Do you remember giving a statement to Officer Anders at the hospital?" He pointed at Amy. She sat up, as if he couldn't see her giant, Charlie Brown head in the front of the gallery.

"Well, I was pretty drunk then, so I don't remember," said

Hernandez.

Anders slumped back in the bench with a hollow thud.

"Do you see any of the men in the courtroom today?" Marks asked, the pitch of his voice rising from bass to tenor.

Hernandez shook his head. "No."

"Do you see anyone who was there that night?" Marks asked.

Hernandez shook his head again. "No. Like I said, I was pretty drunk, so I don't really remember but I definitely don't see anyone here that I recognize today."

Marks looked at the judge, then Hernandez, then Anders, then me.

"May we approach, your Honor?" Marks asked.

Freely motioned with his hand. I stood and started toward the bench. Christy remained seated but I gestured, in turn, to her. This was getting fun.

"Your Honor," Marks wheezed in a loud whisper, "this is blatant witness intimidation!"

Freely grimaced. "What?" He looked at me; I shrugged my shoulders.

"The victim's parents are in the back of the courtroom!" Marks whisper-shouted.

"Yes," said Freely. Nice guy, not terribly sharp.

"Your Honor, these gang trials —"

"I object, your Honor!" I said in my full grown up, outdoor voice. "There has been no showing that there is any gang involvement in this matter. All we've seen so far is a victim who doesn't remember seeing my client at the scene of the crime."

"Mr. Haskell has called the victim's parents for the purpose of intimidation, so Mr. Hernandez sees his parents and won't testify because Mr. Garcia knows who they are!"

Freely sighed.

I continued. "Your Honor, there is no showing of any gang involvement, no showing of any intimidation and frankly, Mr. Garcia is innocent until proven guilty."

Freely scowled. "I'm not very happy with either side of this case right now. Mr. Marks, what do you want me to do?"

I interrupted. "Your Honor, we will move to strike the Commonwealth's case as soon as this the Commonwealth finishes with this witness."

Marks put his hands on his hips, lowered his head.

"Commonwealth moves to nolle prosse the charge," he said out loud.

"Mr. Haskell?" Freely asked, looking over his half glasses.

"No objection," I answered with a smile.

Freely wrote on the summons. "OK, I've entered the nolle prosse." He nodded at the bailiff who moved to the witness stand to retrieve Hernandez.

I turned back to Jorge. Christy followed and I could feel Marks staring at the back of my head.

"OK, Jorge, you are free to go," I said. He was beaming.

"Thank you, Mr. Haskell! You're the best!" He shook my hand.

"Oh, I just have the best clients," I said, with enough fake modesty to make Mr. Rogers puke.

Jorge strode to the back of the courtroom. He slowed as he passed the Hernandezes and smiled at them.

Hernandez himself was by then shuffling toward the door in the paneled wall when he reached his shackled hands up and waved toward the back of the courtroom, "*Hola, mami, papi! No te precupes.*"

I looked in the direction of his wave and saw the middle-aged couple, on their feet by then, wave back. His mother was holding a handkerchief; tears ran down her cheeks. She offered a meek wave in return.

"Mr. and Mrs. Hernandez, you are free to go," said Freely. The interpreter hadn't even gotten to the courtroom yet. "*Ustedes estan libres a ir.*"

They nodded and trudged out of the court. Freely stood and the bailiff commanded us to rise. Freely then exited without a further word.

Marks gathered his papers and files and Anders waited for him at the bar.

"Well, Mizz White," said Marks, "you just got to witness your first gang trial."

"Alleged!" I snickered. Christy just folded her arms. She seemed to do a lot of that.

Marks stalked into my personal space. He smelled like expensive cologne and popcorn farts.

"How do you sleep at night?" he growled.

I smiled. "I sleep like a baby. I wake up screaming every two hours and I shit myself."

Marks faked a smile but pressed even closer. "Very funny, asshole."

Anders grabbed him by the arm. "Let's go, Counselor, before I have to arrest you."

Marks turned on his heel and headed toward the door.

"See you in Hell, Marks," I called after. It was getting crowded in my Hell. Whatever. No more wool sweaters or heavy parkas!

The bailiff had also approached our table. "I'm gonna need you to clear the courtroom. Docket's over."

Christy and I awkwardly took turns going through the swinging gate at the bar.

She pulled up beside me. "What the hell was that?"

"Successful criminal defense?" I grinned.

"Was that . . . was that what Marks said?"

I shrugged. "Every attorney has a right to believe his client. Especially clients who pay cash in advance in small bills."

"You called that kid's parents on purpose so he wouldn't testify!" she shouted at me. She didn't realize that shouting only encourages the incorrigible.

"I subpoenaed Mr. and Mrs. Hernandez because I believed in good faith that they could testify as to Hernandez's whereabouts on the night of the attack. His being present at the crime is a material element of the offense. My client has the right to subpoena witnesses and confront his accuser. What else happens in the courtroom is beyond my control," I said.

"That's disgusting," said Christy. She definitely had her angry face on. Tough shit.

"That's real life, Mizz White. When you get out from behind a desk and get into a courtroom, that's what you see in real life. In real life, people get hurt. People get cheated. People go to jail. My job is to defend my client and I won today. That's all that matters."

"Do you think that was justice in there?" Christy pointed at the courtroom door for emphasis.

"Don't confuse the law with justice, Mizz White. There is precious little of either in the other. Justice? Grow up. There's no justice in that courtroom, or outside of it, for that matter" I said. Sometimes she sounded liked Pollyanna and Pipi Longstocking stuffed into one small body, albeit older and much sexier.

"Mr. Haskell, I am really tired of your condescending, patronizing attitude."

"You want patronizing? Look in a mirror. You know, I just want to do my time with you and get back to life," I said.

"You think you have a life?" she shot back.

I faltered for a moment, a huge mistake. I am really never at a loss for words, as you probably have guessed.

"It is what it is. I don't have a prissy title or an East German weightlifter for a girlfriend like you, but I have a life," I said. I walked with purpose for the stairs.

"Maybe you should look in a mirror…You are a lonely, miserable drunk, Haskell. You hate yourself so much that you can't even see it. And you swim in the deep end of the cesspool because that is where snakes like you feel most comfortable."

"Wow," I said. "You could be the next John Grisham with your flowery command of the English fucking language. Look," I said, stopping and turning. "I'm under a court order to play ball with you, but I don't have to listen to your moralizing. My life is my business. Your job is to make sure

I don't prejudice the rights of any clients. Did I prejudice my client today?"

She paused, and for a moment it looked as if tears were welling up in her eyes. She pressed her lips together tightly, then said, "No, Mr. Haskell, you didn't."

"My client and I are both walking out the front door, so I would say I did my job pretty fucking well."

She nodded slowly. "Yeah, Mr. Haskell, you were a real champ in there today."

You have heard the story of Milt Johns many times before...he writes fiction for a living, but dreams of a career as a petty office bureaucrat. Actually, Milt is a father, husband, attorney, local politician, and author. His publications include two novels, *Patriot Future: A Novel*, Lyford Books, July 1997 and *Fear and Greed*, Amazon Books, February 2012.

He is currently working on his third novel, a legal thriller, and writes poetry when the spirit moves him. Milt is a co-founder and chief operating officer of PJPF, Inc. and a contributing editor to *The Piedmont Journal of Poetry & Fiction*. In his free time, Milt likes to eat, sleep, shoot, and watch college football.

Acknowledgements

Everyone at PJPF would like to thank the writers who have submitted stories, poems, rants, essays, novel excerpts, and dirty jokes over the past four years.

It's been a thrilling journey so far.

Keep them coming, folks. It is our pleasure to work with you.

Sara Brooks
Haymarket, VA
July, 2018